Whether a robe, suit and ti   ave
one design in common—a   y is
those targets show signs oi   ll's-
eye. Every shot hurts, pa.   :es,
and the wounds threaten the survival of the ministry. From a biblical foundation and personal perspective, Beeke and Thompson give practical instructions as to how to handle and heal from the darts of criticism. The old aphorism says that ministers should practice what they preach; to do otherwise makes them hypocrites. It is equally true that ministers should preach what they have first of all practiced; to do otherwise makes them merely theorists. *Pastors and Their Critics* is not theory. The principles outlined are biblical, and they have been proven to work in experience.

—**Michael P. V. Barrett**, Vice President of Academic Affairs, Academic Dean, and Professor of Old Testament, Puritan Reformed Theological Seminary

Receiving criticism is tough. It adds weight to the cross each pastor is called to carry. Its threads are interwoven into every minister's suit. So how can I deal with criticism in a Christlike way? Read this book. It is rich in the two critical ingredients for nurturing Christlike responses in our hearts, thoughts, and actions. It points us to the trainer and deals honestly with our required training. Our Lord Jesus is the trainer. Look to Him. Did people not call Him the chief of the devils? Did they not drive nails through His hands and feet as He prayed for them? Is this not worse than that which anyone ever called or did to you? And by His Spirit this trainer trains His servants in the gymnasium of criticism. We only mature through exercise, and most when it is painful. He must increase and I must decrease is tough for our pride but profitable for our Lord's glory. I know one of the authors, my dear brother, who has been called to exercise in this gymnasium and taught by experience to look to and trust his heavenly trainer. This book is not abstract theory, but reflects the rich benefits of real-life training.

—**James W. Beeke**, Superintendent, British-Columbia–Certified Schools in China; International Educational Consultant

As a young pastor, I received a letter of constructive but rather direct criticism about my preaching from the person who had recommended my name to the pulpit committee of the church! To say that I was stung is to put it mildly. It hurt so badly, I filed it away after one reading and went on about my work. When I ran across the letter again, fifteen years into my ministry there, I realized that every word he said was right and helpful (though I am not sure that I would even have known how to follow his counsel until I had lived a little more life). But it did get me to thinking about criticism, and how to benefit from it and respond to it. This book would have been a help to me then, and will be to you now. To be a pastor, especially in our time, is to be criticized. So how we respond to that criticism, how we process the criticism, how we keep from being defensive or even paralyzed by the criticism, and how we learn and grow from the criticism is all of great significance. We want to be neither despondent nor discouraged but entreatable and correctable. Furthermore, we should learn how to offer criticism in the most God-honoring and helpful way possible. I'm thankful for the hard thinking that has gone into these subjects in this book. I think it will help you as you try to develop "tough skin and a tender heart."
—**Ligon Duncan**, Chancellor and CEO, Reformed Theological Seminary

Like every servant of Christ, I learned early that criticism is part of a minister's labor. But the last few years have brought a level of criticism beyond anything I have ever experienced. In this torrent of controversy and pain, I was asked to review and endorse *Pastors and Their Critics* by Joel Beeke and Nick Thompson. My words here, however, will not be as much an endorsement as a public expression of gratitude to men who have served me so crucially. Their rich work provided comfort, encouragement, correction, and solace that few books ever have. It brought light into a dark season. Pastor, you need the correction and comfort in this book. It is required reading for every minister of the gospel.
—**Heath Lambert**, Senior Pastor, First Baptist Church, Jacksonville, Florida

This book is an invaluable tool for those engaged in the pressures and demands of ministry. Biblically sound, theologically solid, and personally applied, *Pastors and Their Critics* will be a lifeline for every pastor facing the many challenges of ministry.
—**Steven J. Lawson**, President, OnePassion Ministries, Dallas, Texas

I listened to Joel Beeke preaching on "Faithfulness in Dealing with Criticism" at the 2019 Shepherd's Conference, and I said to myself, *Wow, what a blessing! How I wish that sermon could be turned into a book. I would love to read it regularly and commend it to my pastoral friends.* Well, that sermon—and much more—is what you have in this book. Criticism makes and breaks pastors more often than we would like to admit. Often what makes the difference is not the type of criticism itself—whether it is right or wrong—but how a pastor responds to it. This book will help you react to criticism in a biblical way, a way that builds you instead of destroying you. Throw it into your bag when you go on holiday and make it part of your essential reading. You will return to your pastoral ministry a renewed man!
—**Conrad Mbewe**, Pastor, Kabwata Baptist Church, Lusaka, Zambia

As Dr. Beeke's colleague for thirteen years, I've had the privilege of watching him live out this book in real time. I've learned from him how to respond to criticism better and also how to use it to become more Christlike.
—**David Murray**, Pastor; Professor of Old Testament and Practical Theology, Puritan Reformed Theological Seminary; Author, *Reset: Living a Grace-Paced Life in a Burnout Culture*

What a helpful and encouraging book! While our culture conditions us to be overly sensitive, fragile, and defensive, Beeke and Thompson give rich biblical wisdom to fortify and prepare pastors for the inevitable criticism we all face. It should be added to the list of books all pastors and seminarians should read if they are to endure with joy and without bitterness.
—**Michael Reeves**, President and Professor of Theology, Union School of Theology

Receiving just criticism humbly is very difficult. Receiving unjust criticism humbly is equally difficult. Every Christian will be subject to both, and pastors (because they are public figures) are not immune to either. This well-written book will prove lifesaving when the trials come (and come they will). Every pastor, seminarian, office-bearer, and leader will profit from the sound and practical advice given in these pages. I wish I had read this a half century ago. It might have spared me the embarrassment of far too many inappropriate responses on my part. Life changing, Christ exalting, God honoring advice from a pastor whom I love dearly, together with an able seminarian. *Tolle lege.*
—**Derek W. H. Thomas**, Senior Minister, First Presbyterian Church, Columbia, South Carolina; Chancellor's Professor, Reformed Theological Seminary; Teaching Fellow, Ligonier Ministries

When God gave a thorn in the flesh to Paul, it was a messenger of Satan that God knew, and indeed ensured, would do much good to the apostle. In the examples Paul gives of what such thorns might be, he suggests reproaches and distresses (see 2 Cor. 12:10). Criticisms focused on the minister are certainly a distressing reproach, but permitted by God for our increased usefulness, and always accompanied by the promise of all-sufficient grace. This helpful book is a healing balm indicating how we may experience grace—that is, Omnipotence determined to sanctify—during the painful heat of hostility. Every minister and church leader would greatly profit from reading it.
—**Geoffrey Thomas**, Emeritus Pastor, Alfred Place Baptist Church, Aberystwyth, Wales; Conference Speaker; Author

Beeke and Thompson's guide to receiving and responding to criticism is a wonderful gift for the church. From beginning to end it is personally informed, biblically framed, and Christ-centered. If you experience or fear opposition, this little volume is a must read. My only criticism of the book is that it was not published ten years ago.
—**Chad Van Dixhoorn**, Professor of Church History, Westminster Theological Seminary

PASTORS
AND THEIR
CRITICS

PASTORS
AND THEIR
CRITICS

A Guide to Coping with
Criticism in the Ministry

JOEL R. BEEKE and
NICK THOMPSON

P.O. BOX 817 • PHILLIPSBURG • NEW JERSEY 08865-0817

Printed in the United States of America

Library of Congress Cataloging-in-Publication Data

Names: Beeke, Joel R., 1952- author. | Thompson, Nicholas J. 1990- author.
Title: Pastors and their critics : a guide to coping with criticism in the ministry / Joel R. Beeke & Nicholas J. Thompson.
Description: Phillipsburg, New Jersey : P&R Publishing, 2020. | Summary: "Beeke and Thompson provide biblical, practical, and effective tools to handle all types of criticism and to respond with godly wisdom. A vital tool for church leaders and pastors"-- Provided by publisher.
Identifiers: LCCN 2020012196 | ISBN 9781629957524 (paperback) | ISBN 9781629957531 (epub) | ISBN 9781629957548 (mobi)
Subjects: LCSH: Pastoral theology. | Criticism.
Classification: LCC BV4011.3 .B435 2020 | DDC 253/.2--dc23
LC record available at https://lccn.loc.gov/2020012196

For
Jonathan Engelsma,
exemplary friend and peacemaker,
honest and constructive critic, and able leader.
"I thank my God upon every remembrance of you." (Phil. 1:3)
—JRB

For
Mike Waters,
faithful under-shepherd, spiritual father, and wise mentor.
"Be strong in the Lord, and in the power of his might." (Eph. 6:10)
—NJT

CONTENTS

FOREWORD

They say you should never judge a book by its cover. Nor should you gauge its value by its size. True, *Pastors and Their Critics* is brief by comparison with Dr. Joel Beeke's "major" works. But, make no mistake, this is one of the most important books he has written. Indeed, I suspect it may help as many people as his major treatises—not only the ministers, for whom he has written it, but all of us, whether pastors or people.

Perhaps the title leaves a sour taste in your mouth. It should. But this is a book to help pastors—and others—to respond to criticism in a way that shows their mouths and their hearts have been sweetened by the taste of the grace of the Lord Jesus Christ.

Here, then, is a book for the *criticized*, especially the criticized pastor—and what pastor has *never* been criticized? But it is also a book for the *critic*—and who among us has *never* criticized a pastor? To minister to this situation, I know, has been, for Joel Beeke, "the burden of the Lord." He has discharged it here—wisely, I think—in little less than two hundred easily read pages (including a helpful appendix written particularly for seminary students by his able coauthor, Nick Thompson).

Joel Beeke is a theologian and trainer of pastors. He has also been a model and mentor to other pastors because he himself is a pastor. He is, therefore, equipped to give counsel that not only encourages but also challenges us all. There is a message here for every Christian—for the self-pitying pastor ("Why am I being so unjustly criticized?") and the self-assured one ("Surely they can't possibly be criticizing someone with my gifts and position!"), and the critical church member who enjoys having "roast pastor" for Sunday lunch and nibbles at the leftovers during the rest of the week—if we have the honesty to recognize ourselves.

The counsel given in *Pastors and Their Critics* will prepare the seminary student for his calling and give stability to the pastor in his ministry. It underlines the fact that as it was with the Master and his apostles and prophets, so it will be with us: we will experience criticism; we should expect nothing less. Nor should we ever lose sight of our blessings: the high privilege of ministry and people who encourage us. And we should not forget that the Lord can use even hostile instruments to sanctify us and make us fruitful. At the end of the day, the only words that will really matter to us will be our Lord saying, perhaps in a way that brings us to tears of mingled relief and unimaginable bliss, "Well done . . . faithful servant. . . . Enter into the joy of your Lord."

Perhaps I may be allowed a few personal words here, without intruding into the work of the authors. Although by no means the longest standing of Joel Beeke's many friends, we share a friendship that began at a seminar on the theology of John Calvin at Westminster Seminary in the early 1980s. What neither of us could have predicted then was that our meeting would be the beginning of a now four-decades–long friendship. During these years, I have watched the gradual emergence of his ministry, rooted in a self-recognized conservative Dutch-tradition congregation, into one that has reached the ends of the earth.

It is in this context that I am eager to commend *Pastors and Their Critics*. For during these years, I have watched my friend experience the realities he describes in its pages, and much more besides; indeed very much more—experiences calculated to discourage and destroy even strong and able men.

Throughout these years, Joel Beeke has sought to maintain a single eye for God's glory and to model a pastor's concern that all under his care (not to mention many others) should enjoy full assurance of faith in Christ and rejoice in the hope of the glory of God. He has by no means done this alone. As he would be the first to acknowledge, he has been wonderfully supported by his wife Mary, surrounded by his children and his wider family circle, and strengthened by elders and God's people in his church who have devotedly shared his ministry, as well as by a team of fellow workers at Puritan Reformed Theological Seminary and Reformation Heritage Books and a brotherhood of fellow pastors bound up together with him in a common vision and fellowship.

It is, therefore, out of his knowledge of God's Word, God's providence, God's servants, and God's people that the burden to speak and now write on this theme of handling criticism has developed. In *Pastors and their Critics*, he has ably discharged this "burden of the Lord." May the wisdom he shares in it help to humble our pride, strengthen us in our weakness, comfort us in our pain, and make us more deeply sensitive to one another. This is Joel Beeke's desire for his fellow pastors and their people because it is, surely, the desire of the One who is the Bishop and Pastor of the flock for which He laid down His life.

Sinclair B. Ferguson

INTRODUCTION

A LARGELY UNADDRESSED PROBLEM

The day has finally come. You have survived seminary, sustained your ordination exams, and been called to pastor a local church. You experience a profound eagerness in your soul as you step out to follow God's call. You have a hopeful expectation that the sheep entrusted to your care will be built up in faith and holiness through your labors. You have a sanctified aspiration to bring the gospel to lost souls. You have an energy and excitement about the things of God more far-reaching than you have ever experienced before. *What an awesome privilege it is to be a pastor,* you think to yourself.

Soon, however, this sense of ministerial privilege begins to wane. What is the cause of the decline? The prospect that initially appeared bright as the noonday sun has quickly been overshadowed by the clouds of ministerial problems, and in particular, ministerial opposition. On the day of your ordination, dealing with criticism was the farthest thing from your mind. And as you think back on your seminary career, you can't recall ever being taught how to handle such verbal opposition. But here you are, only months into the ministry and already the target of negative words. Perhaps it is your preaching they are unhappy with or the fact that you are not as gregarious as their previous pastor. Whatever it might be, you find yourself receiving verbal backlash. Sure, you expected such opposition from unbelievers. But from your own sheep? The disillusionment begins to sink in. It becomes a daily fight to keep the joys of knowing God, proclaiming His Word, and serving His people from being swallowed up by the harsh words of your congregants or colleagues in the ministry.

This is by no means an uncommon experience. While not every pastor experiences serious criticism from his people in the first months of his ministry, every pastor will meet with it sooner or later. As an old Dutch saying goes, "He who stands in the front will soon be kicked in the rear."

While being criticized is a common pastoral experience, it is, by and large, an unaddressed problem. The majority of men being trained for gospel ministry are not being taught how to handle and respond to such verbal blows. And the consequences of this neglect are grave. A lack of training can quickly lead to disillusionment regarding the ministry, and in far too many cases, even resignation. Being on the receiving end of criticism for any length of time can result in exasperation, insomnia, cynicism, burnout, and even despair.

We have written this book to address this largely unaddressed problem. Helpful material has been written on the subject; as our footnotes will make plain throughout, there are valuable resources dealing with different facets of ministerial critique. But to date, we are not aware of a book that deals comprehensively with the various dimensions of criticism in the Christian ministry from a biblical and Reformed perspective. Such a work is urgently needed for pastors today.

Pastors and Their Critics is broken into four parts. In part one, we lay the biblical foundations for coping with criticism. Broadly tracing the theme of verbal flak from Genesis to Revelation, we seek to ground our understanding of the criticism we face today in its proper biblical and redemptive-historical context. In part two, we provide practical principles for coping with criticism in the ministry. This section comprises the bulk of the book, setting forth the biblical wisdom necessary to receive and respond to criticism in a God-honoring, Christlike way. In part three, we offer practical principles for constructive criticism in the church, discussing how to give criticism as a pastor and how to foster a culture open to criticism in your local congregation. We conclude in part four by setting forth a theological vision for coping with criticism in the gospel ministry, followed by an appendix addressing how to prepare while in seminary for the fires of criticism.

If you are not a pastor and have no aspirations for pastoral ministry, this book is still for you! While we have chosen to focus more narrowly on gospel ministry, the main truths and principles found herein apply to every Christian and every vocation. None of us are exempt from receiving or giving criticism. Thus, we encourage you to take up this book and read!

Pastors and Their Critics has been a joint collaboration, but because of Joel's forty-plus years of pastoral experience, almost all the real-life scenarios found in these pages are his. He rather humorously, yet seriously, asserts that this is finally a book he feels qualified to write because he has had plenty of experience coping with criticism! Rather than continually clarifying this and drawing unnecessary attention to the author, we have decided to only make note when a personal example is from Nick's experience. We trust this will not cause confusion.

As will become clear in the pages ahead, learning to cope with criticism and to give criticism in the Christian ministry is largely a matter of the heart. There are painful lessons we must learn here, and they are seldom learned quickly or easily. For this reason, we encourage you not to breeze through this book in an hour, but to prayerfully ponder and slowly digest it.

As authors, we are grateful for the opportunity to work together on this book and are also thankful for our wives, Mary and Tessa, who helped us rather than criticized us as we pressed on with writing! What a gift a largely affirmative spouse—who also knows how to give constructive criticism—is to a minister (or theological student) who wants to truly grow in serving God faithfully and well! We are grateful to Dave Almack and P&R for pursuing us and cooperating so effectively with us in writing this book. Thanks also to Paul Smalley for his assistance on the first two chapters of this book and to Ray Lanning for doing a helpful editorial pass for us. And finally, thanks to our critics—without them this book would not be what it is and we would not be what we are, by God's grace!

We pray that God will use *Pastors and Their Critics* to work the sanctifying influences of His Word in your soul and ministry, enabling you to endure with joy through the furnace of criticism and come out the better for it. As with any other cross, criticism cannot be so heavy that God's grace cannot sustain you under its weight and enable you to profit from its pain.

PART 1

*BIBLICAL FOUNDATIONS FOR
COPING WITH CRITICISM*

1

OLD TESTAMENT FOUNDATIONS FOR COPING WITH CRITICISM

In waging spiritual warfare, God's people often must advance under withering verbal fire from critics of all kinds. This is true today, and it was true in ancient times. Unjust criticism is woven like a black thread throughout covenant history.[1] While it is not possible to provide a comprehensive biblical theology of criticism in these pages, we want to present some of the most striking Old Testament examples. As we study them, we discover principles for coping with criticism that apply to all who would follow the cross-bearing Messiah.

PRELAPSARIAN CRITICISM: GOD

Who was the first target of unjust criticism? The answer may surprise you. The earliest appearance of character-distorting

---

1. While this book addresses both constructive and destructive criticism, this chapter will focus primarily on the latter as it is found throughout God's old covenant revelation. There are certainly many examples of constructive critique found in the Old Testament. One thinks, for example, of the prophetic witness critiquing and rebuking Israel that she might be brought to repentance for her covenant-breaking.

verbal abuse was actually in the garden of Eden. And the object of this destructive criticism was God Himself.

Having created a cosmos in the space of six days, God created man as the crowning jewel of His creation. He placed Adam in a garden paradise to tend and keep it as a priest-king, generously providing His image-bearing creature with a vast array of trees and fruits to eat from and commanding him not to eat only from one tree (see Gen. 2:15–17). In the bond of the covenant of life, God and man enjoyed perfect fellowship unhindered from sin and mistrust.

Into this prelapsarian bliss, however, a serpent intruded himself. He was a crafty beast, the vehicle through which Satan would carry out his destructive scheme to deface the glory of God. How would he do this? By words—deceitful, godless words. The chatter by which he seduced our first parents was in the form of criticism. And though spoken to man, this criticism was directed squarely at God Himself. The serpent's temptation came in the form of a lie about God, attacking "both God's generosity and his integrity."[2]

He began with a seemingly innocent question: "Yea, hath God said, Ye shall not eat of every tree of the garden?" (Gen. 3:1). But this question was anything but innocent. By it he not only questioned the veracity of God's Word ("Has God *really* said?"), but he also subtly distorted the nature of the prohibition. God had not forbidden our first parents from eating of *every* tree in Eden. He had clearly told them, "Of every tree of the garden thou mayest freely eat," keeping from them only the tree of the knowledge of good and evil (Gen. 2:16–17). The serpent's question portrayed God as stingy and restrictive.

2. Sinclair B. Ferguson, *The Whole Christ: Legalism, Antinomianism, & Gospel Assurance—Why the Marrow Controversy Still Matters* (Wheaton, IL: Crossway, 2016), 69.

Satan began with a pallid criticism easily undetected, but when Eve's response indicated that he had succeeded in planting seeds of doubt in her mind concerning God's word and character, his verbal attack on God became undeniably bold. He now asserted in no uncertain terms that God was a liar, emphatically declaring, "Ye shall not surely die" (Gen. 3:4). The serpent "openly accuses God of falsehood," writes Calvin, "for he asserts that the word by which death was denounced is false and delusive."[3] And the reason given by the deceiver as to why God lied was that He did not want mankind to rival His deity (see Gen. 3:5). Satan was in essence saying, "God is one whose motives make His word unreliable. He lies from selfishness."[4] A major question mark was placed over the trustworthiness of His word just by marring His character. The thrice holy God was slandered as a restrictive, envious, unloving liar.

When we suffer from the false accusations and character-disfiguring words of others, our minds should be quick to return to this grim garden conspiracy wherein our Creator was vilified by the serpent. It is one thing for a creature to be criticized unjustly by another creature, but it is the atrocity of atrocities for the Creator of all things to be verbally assassinated by a mere creature. The first person ever criticized was the only One who has nothing in Him worthy of criticism. When we are criticized, even falsely so, there is usually at least a sliver of truth in what is being said. This sliver of truth gives the criticism clout. But not so with God. "God is not a man, that he should lie" (Num. 23:19). He "is light, and in him is no darkness at all" (1 John 1:5). There is not the slightest blemish in the divine character worthy of criticism. In the garden we find verbal injustice in its most concentrated form.

3. John Calvin, *Commentaries on the Book of Genesis,* trans. John King (Grand Rapids: Eerdmans, 1948), 150 (exposition of Gen. 3:4).
4. Geerhardus Vos, *Biblical Theology: Old and New Testaments* (Edinburgh: Banner of Truth, 1975), 36.

The first account of abusive words in covenant history resulted in the fall of mankind, which in turn became the source of all destructive criticism thereafter.[5] What we find as we read through the Old Testament is a history littered with the Serpent's deceit. And we can be certain it will continue so long as the cosmic war between Satan and the Savior continues (see Gen. 3:15). As you face unjust criticism in the ministry, it is imperative for you to understand that your suffering is not a personal, isolated experience, but a part of the great redemptive-historical drama whose chief antagonist is the devil (literally "the slanderer").

This truth ought to be comforting, though it is not always easy to cling to in times of criticism. I must confess that I've had numerous times in my life where I felt more alone than taken up in this great redemptive-historical drama. There was a season in my thirties when Satan became very real to me, and I felt attacked from all quarters by him and a few colleagues. I remember vividly telling the Lord aloud in a desperate tone of voice that there was no minister on earth attacked at that moment like I was. Certainly no one had experienced what I was going through! Loneliness, self-pity, the reality of Satan, and a sense of desperation seemed overwhelming to me. I felt the rushing river of satanic criticism would never be calm again. There was no end in sight. Nights were often sleepless, though at times God would give me some respite. One night in particular, when sleep was impossible until around 4:30 a.m., two texts entered my mind that served me better than any sleeping pill ever could do: "For we have not an high priest which cannot be touched with the feeling of our infirmities; but was in all points tempted like as we are, yet without sin" (Heb. 4:15) and "There hath no temptation taken you but such as is common to man: but God is faithful,

5. All constructive criticism likewise has its source in the fall since there would be no fault to be found in man prior to sin.

who will not suffer you to be tempted above that ye are able; but will with the temptation also make a way to escape, that ye may be able to bear it" (1 Cor. 10:13). Then I saw and understood my part in the redemptive-historical drama and was able to gain the victory over the devil—at least for a few weeks! What a blessing that God's Word is stronger than Satan's actions!

PRIESTLY CRITICISM: MOSES AND AARON

The Serpent in his craftiness strategically aims his disparaging lies at the anointed leaders of God's people. Few Old Testament leaders suffered from these fiery darts of Satan to the degree that Moses did. From day one of his ministry, he faced seething verbal abuse from his own people (see Ex. 5:21). Within a week of their mighty deliverance from Egyptian bondage, the people were venting complaints toward their God-appointed deliverer (see Ex. 15:24; 16:2–3). Their forty years of wandering in the wilderness were marked by recurrent floods of unjust criticism hatefully aimed at this man of God, even by his own brother and sister (see Num. 12:1–3; 14:1–4).

In Numbers 16 we are introduced to four men, a Levite named Korah and three Reubenites named Dathan, Abiram, and On. These men united with other members of the covenant community in order to assault the leadership of Moses and Aaron (see vv. 1–2). Filled with envy and hatred, they issued devastating critiques of the ministries of these men of God.

First, Korah and his band of followers uttered accusations against Aaron, claiming that he had abused his authority and arrogantly exalted himself above the people: "Ye take too much upon you, seeing all the congregation are holy, every one of them, and the Lord is among them: wherefore then lift ye up yourselves above the congregation of the Lord?" (v. 3). Notice the truth that is carefully twisted in order to undermine Aaron's high priestly ministry. Korah's premise is true; his accusation is false. Israel was indeed a holy nation (see Ex. 19:6), indicated in the immediately preceding context by the commandment to make fringes on the peoples' garments to remind them of their part in the covenant, to do all His commandments and be holy unto their God (see Num. 15:37–41). There is truth here, but it is abused, or used to a bad end.[6] The "set-apartness" of the people did not eliminate God-given order or authority structures among the people. The Lord Himself had called Aaron (see Heb. 5:4) as the representative high priest of His people. Thus, we find here "an expression of unjust criticism. . . . an unkind and untrue allegation" leveled against Aaron.[7] Such verbal abuse typically warps some form of truth. Scripture may be wrested or handled deceitfully to make it appear that God is on the side of the critic. As leaders of God's people, we must exercise great wisdom to discern whether "biblical" criticism is truly biblical.

What led Korah to distort the truth and wrongly oppose his spiritual leader? He was jealous of Aaron's position. Ironically, Korah was a Levite, possessing a noble vocation and the high responsibility of caring for the tabernacle of God. The two hundred fifty men with him were "princes" (KJV) or the "chiefs of the congregation" (Num. 16:2 ESV). These were not men of low estate or "sons of Belial." "It is not those at the bottom of the heap who rebel against God's order," comments Iain Duguid, "but those who are close to the top and who think they ought themselves to be at the top."[8] This is why after highlighting the uncontested privilege of being a Levite, Moses asked, "And seek ye the priesthood also?" (v. 10). Korah was hankering after that

6. This, of course, was the tactic of the serpent in the garden.
7. Reymond Brown, *The Message of Numbers: Journey to the Promised Land,* The Bible Speaks Today (Downers Grove, IL: IVP Academic, 2002), 145.
8. Iain M. Duguid, *Numbers: God's Presence in the Wilderness,* Preaching the Word (Wheaton, IL: Crossway, 2006), 201.

which was not his, hungry for more power and jealous of those whom God had placed over him. Truly, "jealousy is cruel as the grave" (Song 8:6).

At this point the flood of unjust criticism had only begun. Dathan and Abiram, though they had schemed together with Korah, were not willing to oppose Moses and Aaron face-to-face. They freely gossiped about their leaders behind their backs, but left the "dirty work" of confrontation to Korah.[9] So Moses called for them, but they refused to appear before him (see Num. 16:12). The reasons given came in the form of scathing criticism directed, this time, at Moses. They accused him of murder, bringing them out of Egypt (which, in verse 14, they tellingly called "a land that floweth with milk and honey") only to kill them in the wilderness. And having done that, Moses had aspired to make himself a "prince" over them (v. 13). He had moreover failed to bring them to the promised land. Though others might be blinded by his deception, they would not be duped by his empty promises (see v. 14).

The reality was that this generation of Israelites would die in the wilderness; they would never reach the promised land. But was this due to a failure on the part of Moses? Had Moses deceived them? Absolutely not. They could not enter Canaan because of their own unbelief (see Ps. 95:7–11; Heb. 4:1–11). Rather than owning their sin and repenting of it, they point the finger at their leader. "Moses is a deceitful, power-hungry murderer," they propounded. What devastating deception!

We learn here that hidden beneath the surface of destructive criticism are sinful motivations. Such hateful speech may be fueled by an envious hunger for promotion and prestige (Korah) or an attempt to appease one's conscience by shifting the blame

9. Gordon Keddie, *Numbers: According to Promise,* Welwyn Commentary Series (Darlington, UK: Evangelical Press, 2010), 114.

of one's own sins to another (Dathan and Abiram). But it never comes out of nowhere. Leaders must be skilled in getting to issues of the heart, as Moses was, helping opponents to see that in their deceit, they are actually siding with the Serpent and against God (see Num. 16:11).

Before responding to his critics, however, it is notable that in both instances Moses first went to God.[10] After Korah's initial verbal assault, Moses "fell upon his face" (v. 4), indicating his humble submission to and dependence on God. Again, after Dathan and Abiram's brutal denunciation, Moses turned in righteous indignation to the Lord (see v. 15). He committed his case to the Lord, seeking His help and wisdom, and only then did he turn to his critics and address them. His prayerful resignation and evident fear of the Lord are exemplary for those who would lead God's people today. We must be slow to rebuke our critics and quick to humble ourselves before God in earnest prayer.

God vindicated His servants in response to their petitions. He caused the earth to devour Korah, Dathan, and Abiram, along with their households (see v. 32). He also consumed with fire the two hundred fifty leaders who had accompanied them in their slanderous escapade (see v. 35). You would think such a manifestation of divine judgment would bring an end to Israel's destructive criticism of their leaders, but they did not get the message. Rather, the next day the entire congregation now murmured against Moses and Aaron, accusing them of wholesale murder: "Ye have killed the people of the Lord" (v. 41). This again led to judgment, but remarkably, Moses and Aaron interceded on behalf of the people, saving the entire congregation from being wiped out by divine wrath (see vv. 43–49). In so doing, they

10. This is characteristic of Moses's entire ministry. It seems that at every point where he is recorded being unjustly criticized, he immediately goes to prayer (see Ex. 5:22–23; 15:25; Num. 14:5), or the Lord immediately intervenes in the situation (see Ex. 16:4; Num. 12:4).

exhibited profound humility and love toward their persecutors. If we would honor the Lord when receiving unjust verbal abuse, we must do the same.

POLITICAL CRITICISM: DAVID

David was another anointed leader among God's people who was no stranger to the slander of the Serpent. One of the darkest times in David's life was the rebellion of his son Absalom, which resulted in nothing less than his attempt to kill David and usurp the throne. When news of this rebellion reached Jerusalem, David and his servants fled the city in great distress (see 2 Sam. 15). Part of the humiliation of this debacle was the knowledge that David had brought this suffering on himself by his own sins (see 2 Sam. 12:10).

To make matters even worse, as David fled from Jerusalem, a kinsman of the late King Saul named Shimei came out and erupted against David like "a human volcano."[11] He hurled both words and rocks at the refugees, though it seems from a safe distance (see 2 Sam. 16:5–13). He cursed David as a "bloody man" (a person guilty of bloodshed or violence) and "man of Belial" (a worthless, wicked person), and said, "The Lord hath returned upon thee all the blood of the house of Saul, in whose stead thou hast reigned; and the Lord hath delivered the kingdom into the hand of Absalom thy son: and, behold, thou art taken in thy mischief, because thou art a bloody man" (2 Sam. 16:7–8). Shimei's criticism was especially unfair in that he accused David of doing the very thing that David had not done. Saul, Ishbosheth, and Abner were all at times within the reach of David's vengeance, but David touched none of them.

---

11. Dale Ralph Davis, *2 Samuel: Out of Every Adversity*, Focus on the Bible Commentary (Ross-shire, UK: Christian Focus Publications, 2002), 202.

Such unfair criticism is often an irresistible bait for bitter self-justification. When we suffer from abusive words or false accusations, our anger tends to flare up much more easily. Embittered within ourselves, we can respond savagely to those who abuse and irritate us. In fact, David's servant Abishai answered Shimei insult for insult ("this dead dog," v. 9) and offered to remove his head with a sword—and it would have been no surprise had David permitted it. The king would have been justified in having Shimei put to death, for the law of God says, "Thou shalt not . . . curse the ruler of thy people" (Ex. 22:28). However, David did not exact retribution because greater than any personal vindication David might have wanted was his conviction that God was ordering this event in His sovereign mercy and chastening love.

First, David remembered *God's sovereignty over all things*, saying, "Let him curse, because the LORD hath said unto him, Curse David" (2 Sam. 16:10). Not once but twice, David said, "Let him alone, and let him curse; for the LORD hath bidden him" (v. 11). David was not suggesting that God had directly spoken to Shimei and commanded him to deliver this unjust criticism. Instead, he recognized that God had decreed all things, even the verbal abuse of his enemies. God had ordered the event, so it came as discipline from the Lord, though the sin involved was from Shimei and Satan.[12] While Shimei had no right to treat David in such a way, God had the right to bring this affliction on David, and David bowed under God's sovereignty, acknowledging that this criticism was from the Lord, as well as justifying the

12. John Gill wrote that God did this "not by way of command, or a precept of his; for to curse the ruler of the people is contrary to the word and law of God (Ex. 22:28); nor by any operation of his Spirit moving and exciting him to it; for the operations of the Spirit are to holiness, and not to sin; but by the secret providence of God ordering, directing, and overruling all circumstances relative to this affair." *Gill's Commentary* (1852–1854; repr., Grand Rapids: Baker, 1980), 2:285.

Lord, approving the Lord, and even clinging to the Lord. How often in moments of severe criticism we fail to bow under God's sovereignty—just when we need to do so the most! And it is precisely that failure that often brings us into restlessness, distress, and agony. No wonder Martin Luther, who was often criticized on every side, said letting God be God is more than half of all true religion!

Second, David responded meekly because he entrusted himself to *God's omniscient mercy and overruling justice*: "It may be that the LORD will look on mine affliction,[13] and that the LORD will requite me good for his cursing this day" (2 Sam. 16:12). God had promised to treat David and his offspring with fatherly love (see 2 Sam. 7:14–15), and David submitted to God's discipline with a childlike trust in his Father's goodness. It was God's Word rather than Shimei's words that controlled how David responded. William Blaikie said, "It was better to bear the wrong, and leave the rectifying of it in God's hands; for God detests unfair dealing, and when His servants receive it He will look to it and redress it in His own time and way."[14]

These two principles are powerful means of enabling us to respond to criticism in a manner that shows "true greatness,"[15]

13. There is a textual issue here. The Masoretic text reads "my iniquity." The marginal reading of the Hebrew text, appearing in some other Hebrew manuscripts, is "my eye," which was interpreted by rabbis as "my tears." The ancient translations such as the LXX and most English translations read "my affliction" (Davis, *2 Samuel*, 203–4). The phrase "look upon iniquity" does not seem to appear in Scripture; the expression "look upon affliction" appears in a number of texts referring to God's compassion (see Gen. 29:32; 31:42; Ex. 3:7; 4:31; Deut. 26:7; 1 Sam. 1:11; 2 Kings 14:26; Neh. 9:9; Pss. 9:13; 25:18; 31:7; 119:153; Lam. 1:7, 9), and therefore is the most likely reading.

14. W. G. Blaikie, *The Second Book of Samuel* (1893; repr., Minneapolis: Klock and Klock, 1978), 247.

15. Joyce G. Baldwin, *1 & 2 Samuel: An Introduction and Commentary,* Tyndale Old Testament Commentaries (Downers Grove, IL: Inter-Varsity, 1988), 263.

indeed, "a strong resemblance to the meek resignation of Jesus."[16] We learn to see past the people who harass us and recognize the hand of God controlling all and the heart of God that will make everything right for His people. It is not easy to do this when the wicked pelt us with their verbal stones, but God's promises give us everything we need to persevere in godliness.

Even after he returned victorious to Jerusalem, David did not exact vengeance on Shimei. Rejecting their counsel against Shimei, David called the bloodthirsty "sons of Zeruiah" (Abishai, Joab, and Asahel) his "adversaries" (2 Sam. 19:22). He implied that those who would repay insults with vengeful words and deeds were just as much his enemies as Shimei was.

A real test of the godliness of our response to criticism is how we treat our enemies after the tables are turned—when they no longer have power over us, but we over them (see Ps. 141:5–6). Will we show them grace and mercy then? Or will we take the opportunity to repay them with the same verbal lashing that they gave to us? It is one thing to pass the test of meekness when you are powerless to counterattack. It is another thing to pass the test of magnanimity when your enemy cowers before you. If we use our power to avenge our honor, then we dishonor ourselves.

For several years I had a difficult time coping with one of my members who would come frequently to my study to sharply criticize something I said in a recent sermon. He was the kind of member who would say, "At 37 minutes and 24 seconds into your sermon, you said X, but don't you think it would have been better and more biblical if you had said Y?" He came so often and was so detailed that I must confess that, apart from the times that he was right, it all became rather disheartening. Finally, I determined that the next time he came, I was going to ask him to save

16. Blaikie, *Second Book of Samuel*, 246.

all his criticisms and come to me with them no more than four times a year. When he sat down this time, however, he said, "You must be weary with me coming to you so often with criticisms of your sermons. Well, I want to confess to you that I have come in the wrong spirit, and I don't know if there is any room in your heart to possibly forgive me, but I want you to know I am very sorry." I jumped up immediately, and said, "Stand up, brother! I forgive you completely"—and I gave him a bear hug that I hope he never forgets!

Don't make your enemies cower before you when they confess their faults. Receive them in the spirit that your heavenly Father receives you when you confess your faults to Him in Christ—immediately, freely, and fully He forgives you (see Ps. 32:5)! Meekness readily forgives our critics; when we are meek we remember what sinners we are as well.

But meekness does not mean standing by and letting the wicked have the upper hand; rather, it is the conviction that though "the wicked plotteth against the just, and gnasheth upon him with his teeth," nevertheless, "the LORD shall laugh at him: for he seeth that his day is coming" (Ps. 37:12–13).

POSTEXILIC CRITICISM: NEHEMIAH

Aaron, Moses, and David suffered unjust criticism from those within the covenant community, but often it is those in the world who slander the Lord's anointed.[17] For an example of this we turn to the great leader of God's postexilic people, Nehemiah. Exercising a remarkable combination of prayer and leadership skill, Nehemiah mobilized the Israelites who had returned to the ruins

17. Aaron, Moses, and David also knew what it was to be criticized from outside Israel. See, for example, Pharaoh's false accusations of Moses and Aaron in Exodus 5:4–5 and Goliath's hateful critique of David in 1 Samuel 17:43–44.

of Jerusalem to rebuild the city walls (see Neh. 1–2)—a strategic act for the future security, honor, and prosperity of God's people. The inhabitants of Jerusalem responded to Nehemiah's call with great unity, each family taking on a portion of the wall as its responsibility (see Neh. 3). Their progress, however, did not please the Samaritans (who professed to worship Israel's God) and the Gentiles living nearby.

Sanballat the Horonite, governor of Samaria, was enraged at the news and scoffed, saying, "What do these feeble Jews? will they fortify themselves? will they sacrifice? will they make an end in a day? will they revive the stones out of the heaps of the rubbish which are burned?" (Neh. 4:2). Tobiah the Ammonite joined in the mockery, saying, "Even that which they build, if a fox go up, he shall even break down their stone wall" (Neh. 4:3). Here we find the weapon of ridicule deployed, which "needs no factual ammunition; not even argument."[18] Yet ridicule "is effective because it strikes at the hidden insecurity or weaknesses which almost everybody has."[19]

Notice that this criticism attacked every aspect of the work:

- the incapacity of the workers ("feeble");
- the impossibility of their physical and spiritual goals ("fortify" and "sacrifice");
- the constraints of their timetable ("in a day");
- the sufficiency of their resources ("heaps of the rubbish which are burned"); and
- the quality of their workmanship ("a fox . . . shall even break it down").

18. Derek Kidner, *Ezra & Nehemiah: An Introduction and Commentary*, Tyndale Old Testament Commentaries (Downers Grove, IL: Inter-Varsity, 1979), 90.

19. James M. Boice, *Nehemiah: Learning to Lead* (Old Tappan, NJ: Fleming H. Revell, 1990), 77.

Sanballat and Tobiah literally had nothing good to say; the whole project was a disaster. Perhaps you have encountered such devastating criticism: not a constructive assessment of strengths and weaknesses, but a wholesale assault that makes it look stupid to even try. This is one of Satan's key tactics against God's people. Gerald Bilkes writes, "Rather than issuing an all-out assault on us, which we might more easily recognize, Satan tries to intimidate us psychologically and spiritually. This effective weapon is often successful in immobilizing believers."[20]

The irony of the text is that this devastating criticism was provoked by the budding success of the wall's reconstruction (see Neh. 4:1). "The first thing we should know," advises James Boice, "if we are trying to do something worthwhile and are being opposed, is that it is because we are achieving something."[21] Satan rarely attacks our spiritual failures—he does not need to.

A few weeks before working on this chapter, I received an anonymous email in which the author signed his name "Theophilus" (Greek, "He who loves God"). The letter was one of the most scathing I have ever received in my life. It was so bad that I don't want to tell you what it said, in case you would think part or all of it might be true! In fact, I told my wife that I didn't even dare read it to her. I thought I knew who it was from, but it can be tormenting not to know for sure. I tried to pray about it without much success, so I called a very close friend who knows me better than anyone else in the world besides my wife. When I read the letter to him, he said to me, "This is straight from the bottom of hell. There is no truth in it. It doesn't sound like you whatsoever. Throw it away immediately, and get back to work right away. Don't let any Saballat or Tobiah keep you from doing

20. Gerald M. Bilkes, *Memoirs of the Way Home: Ezra and Nehemiah as a Call to Conversion* (Grand Rapids: Reformation Heritage Books, 2013), 107.
21. Boice, *Nehemiah*, 72.

the Lord's work." I followed my friend's advice to throw it away, praying for forgiveness if any part of this letter (God forbid!) was true. Then I went straight back to work.

Notice that Nehemiah does the same thing. The text does not record any direct response from Nehemiah. He had answered them already by his diligence in performing the necessary leadership tasks in this great building project. He may have felt it a waste of words to reply to such mean-spirited criticism. However, he lifted his voice to God: "Hear, O our God; for we are despised: and turn their reproach upon their own head, and give them for a prey in the land of captivity: and cover not their iniquity, and let not their sin be blotted out from before thee: for they have provoked thee to anger before the builders" (Neh. 4:4–5). Nehemiah prayed for the covenant-keeping God to vindicate His people and punish the wicked who opposed them. Then he got back to work: "So built we the wall . . . for the people had a mind to work" (Neh. 4:6).

There are situations when it is a waste of time to defend yourself before men. The best defense is to appeal to God and keep on working. If people have sincere and significant questions about a project, then by all means answer them honestly and courteously, but if they are only out to slander and obstruct, don't let them slow you down. Don't be distracted. Keep your eyes on the Lord and your hands busy in His work.

On top of his verbal abuse, Sanballat repeatedly attempted to lure Nehemiah away from the worksite in order to do him harm, but Nehemiah wisely replied that he was too busy to come down (see Neh. 6:1–4). Finally, Sanballat sent Nehemiah an open letter accusing him of stirring up the Jews to rebel against the Persian empire and set himself up as their king (see Neh. 6:5–7). This is a typical move by hostile, destructive critics (as opposed to constructive critics): if their criticisms of the project fail to impede it, then they shift to personal attacks on its leader, in this case with dangerous political implications. These were charges based on unnamed sources and altogether false.

How did Nehemiah respond? He denied the charges (see v. 8), but recognized that the accusations had stirred up fear, and so gave himself to more prayer: "Now therefore, O God, strengthen my hands" (v. 9). When personal attacks lead to debilitating anxiety, it is wise to pray for more grace to persevere in boldness and faithfulness. What resources we find through prayer!

The result was that the wall was finished in just fifty-two days, the enemies of Israel were discouraged and defeated, and God was publicly glorified as the One who had made it all happen (see vv. 15–16). What followed was nothing less than biblical reformation, covenant renewal, and the restoration of true worship among the people of God.

In the midst of fierce criticism, it strengthens us to remember that if we do not grow weary in well-doing, we will reap a harvest in due time (see Gal. 6:9). We might feel we are hacking our way through a forest of thorns one step at a time, but by our weary arm and many wounds we are blazing a trail for others to follow. Who knows how God might use that trail in the future? He can "do exceeding abundantly above all that we ask or think" (Eph. 3:20). Christ is not idle, but works in and through His servants even to the end of the age (see Matt. 28:20). Persevere in the work, hope in the Lord, and—like Moses, David, and Nehemiah—you will find that God remembers you for good.

2

CHRISTOLOGICAL FOUNDATIONS FOR COPING WITH CRITICISM

The age-old warfare between the Serpent and Eve's seed reached its climax in the incarnation and death of the Son of God. All of covenant history was hastening forward to this moment when, born as a son of Adam, Christ would come to reverse the sin-induced curse on mankind and to destroy the slanderous devil and all his works. Greater than Moses, David, and Nehemiah, He came as the anointed Prophet, Priest, and King to bring His people out of bondage and exile and into the land of God's favor. But the manner in which Jesus liberated His people and crushed the Serpent's head was altogether unexpected. He destroyed the powers of darkness through death on a Roman cross, bearing His people's sins in order to set them free.

Christ's death not only purchased redemption, but also provided a pattern for His disciples to follow. Peter writes, "For even hereunto were ye called: because Christ also suffered for us, leaving us an example, that ye should follow his steps" (1 Peter 2:21). The suffering Messiah is not only our representative; He is also our exemplar. Following in the steps of the cross-bearing Christ is not optional for those who claim to be His disciples (see Luke 9:23).

What we might not realize is that much of Christ's suffering consisted in enduring verbal abuse, or "contradiction of sinners" (Heb. 12:3). This should not come as a surprise given that one of Satan's primary weapons in overcoming the Lord's anointed ones is deceitful speech. Peter highlights this ugly reality: "Who did no sin, neither was guile found in his mouth: who, *when he was reviled, reviled not again*; when he suffered, he threatened not; but committed himself to him that judgeth righteously" (1 Peter 2:22–23). The verb translated "to be reviled" means to be reproached, insulted, spoken of disrespectfully, or falsely accused.[1] Peter uses the same root word when he exhorts believers not to render "evil for evil, or *railing for railing*: but contrariwise blessing; knowing that ye are thereunto called, that ye should inherit a blessing" (1 Peter 3:9).

If Jesus came to bring an end to evil, why would he quietly bear such assaults? This forbearance may seem utterly contrary to the image of a holy warrior fighting against evil. It may have the appearance of giving in to evil rather than warring against it. Jonathan Edwards recognized this problem, and he argued that "many persons seem to be quite mistaken concerning the nature of Christian fortitude," which is a very different thing "from a brutal fierceness, or the boldness of beasts of prey."[2] On the contrary, Edwards said the power of a Christian is first and foremost shown in ruling himself and conquering his own sin and fear, not in conquering other people. Edwards wrote, "Though Christian fortitude appears, in withstanding and counteracting the enemies that are without us; yet it much more appears, in resisting

---

1. "λοιδορέω, etc." in *Theological Dictionary of the New Testament*, ed. Gerhard Kittel, Geoffrey W. Bromiley, and Gerhard Friedrich (Grand Rapids: Eerdmans, 1967), 4:293–94.

2. Jonathan Edwards, *Religious Affections*, in *The Works of Jonathan Edwards*, vol. 2, ed. John E. Smith (New Haven: Yale University Press, 1959), 350.

and suppressing the enemies that are within us; because they are our worst and strongest enemies, and have greatest advantage against us. The strength of the good soldier of Jesus Christ, appears in nothing more, than in steadfastly maintaining the holy calm, meekness, sweetness, and benevolence of his mind, amidst all the storms, injuries, strange behavior, and surprising acts and events of this evil and unreasonable world."[3]

No one exercised more self-control and steadfastness under hostile fire than Jesus. Christ is a model for us of how to respond in the best way to criticism of the worst kind. He set the highest example to be found in human history of showing meekness toward one's critics. Christ's response to criticism recorded in the gospel accounts ought to shape our minds, affections, and wills as we undergo verbal flak in the gospel ministry.

THE SILENCE OF THE LAMB

Betrayed, arrested, forsaken by friends, and brought before a court composed of His most bitter enemies, the Lord Jesus found Himself confronted by witnesses speaking lies against Him (see Matt. 26:49, 55–61). Two liars accused Him of threatening to destroy the most sacred site of Israel, the temple—twisting the words by which He predicted His death and resurrection (see John 2:20–22). Malicious critics often use our own well-meant words as weapons against us. It was a nightmarish situation, yet Christ knew that it would come. One might have expected Him to prepare a brilliant speech in His defense. His previous skirmishes with the Sadducees and Pharisees showed that no one could defeat Him in a war of words. Yet amazingly, in the face of His accusers, "Jesus held his peace" (Matt. 26:63). Calvin wrote, "Having been appointed to be a sacrifice, he had thrown aside all

3. Edwards, 2:350.

anxiety about defending himself."[4] Christ set His mind on doing the will of God and fulfilling His mission, and He refused to be distracted from it.

Christ's Suffering Clothed in Meekness

When the Sanhedrin condemned Jesus to death, the members of the court took turns spitting in His face, buffeting Him, striking Him, and taunting Him (see Matt. 26:67–68). When morning came, they took him to Pontius Pilate and accused Him of claiming to be a king, an act of rebellion against the empire. Again, this was grossly unfair, for Jesus had never sought political power or earthly kingship (see John 6:15), but promoted proper submission to the civil powers (see Matt. 22:21). This slander misrepresented His entire teaching about the nature of God's kingdom in this age (see Matt. 13). Once more, Jesus said nothing, much to the astonishment of the Roman governor (see Matt. 27:12–14). No doubt Pilate was used to seeing adversaries hotly accuse each other of the worst of crimes while defending themselves to the bitter end. But this quiet, peaceful Man stood before him in silence while such charges were laid against Him. Pilate possessed no categories for such undisturbed meekness.

It might be argued that Christ's situation was unique because of His unique commission as God's suffering Servant. However, while the spiritual torments of Christ under the curse of God's law were unique (see Gal. 3:13), the social rejection and physical afflictions He suffered are shared by His followers, albeit to varying degrees. Verbal abuse comes with the territory of cross-bearing. Paul wrote concerning himself and the other apostles, "Being reviled, we bless; being persecuted, we suffer it: being

4. John Calvin, *Commentary on a Harmony of the Evangelists: Matthew, Mark, and Luke,* ed. William Pringle (Grand Rapids: Eerdmans, 1948), 3:255 (exposition of Matt. 26:62).

defamed, we intreat: we are made as the filth of the world, and are the offscouring of all things unto this day" (1 Cor. 4:12–13). Christ said that His kingdom belongs to those who "are persecuted for righteousness' sake," and went on to warn His followers that "men shall revile you . . . and say all manner of evil against you falsely, for my sake" (Matt. 5:10–11). Living a godly life in a wicked world will provoke opposition, causing people to talk about us (see 2 Tim. 3:12). Christ did not endure the cross to exempt us from our crosses, but to demonstrate for us how to be more than conquerors as we share in His sufferings. Like Him, we overcome when we evidence that doing God's will and fulfilling our calling is more important to us than life itself (see Acts 20:24).

Pilate, having learned that Christ came from Galilee, sent Him to Herod Antipas, the "tetrarch" or ruler of that region of Palestine. Herod asked Jesus many questions, hoping to see Him perform a miracle. The priests and scribes stood by, vehemently accusing Christ of wrongdoing. Again Jesus said nothing. So Herod and his men of war subjected Christ to mockery, "arrayed him in a gorgeous robe," and returned Him to Pilate (Luke 23:6–11).

Receiving Him back, Pilate "scourged Jesus," that is, administered a severe whipping or lashing (Matt. 27:26). Then Pilate's soldiers stripped Jesus of His own clothes and arrayed Him in a scarlet robe, while plaiting a crown of thorns for His head and giving Him a reed to hold in His right hand as a scepter. They proceeded to hail Him sarcastically as "King of the Jews," first kneeling before Him and then spitting on Him and beating Him over the head (Matt. 27:27–30). In the face of this infamous hatred and injustice, there is no record of Jesus uttering a word of protest. His silence is striking once more. Judas and his cohorts who came to arrest Christ witnessed his kingly power when He cast them backward to the ground with His self-identification of

"I AM." But then Christ showed lamblike submission in allowing Himself to be arrested, bound, and led away in silence to His various judges, including Pilate, before whom His silence became so astonishing that Pilate himself marveled at it. Christ was silent, patiently entrusting Himself "to him that judgeth righteously" (1 Peter 2:23).

What tremendous courage is to be found in meditating on Christ's meek endurance when we too face criticism, even criticism that threatens our income, our prospect, or our lives! Paul prays for the persecuted saints in Thessalonica that the Lord would "direct [their] hearts into the love of God, and into the patience of Christ" (2 Thess. 3:5).[5] The word translated "patience" literally means *enduring* under difficult circumstances.[6] Paul is praying that God would cause these saints to think in a focused and sustained way about how Christ patiently endured persecution, so that by faith in Him they might do the same. When we meditate with belief on Christ, the Spirit meets with us and enables us to say, "He suffered for me, and now I will suffer this criticism for Him. God has vindicated His Son, and God will vindicate me one day as well."

After being lifted up on the cross, Christ was not left alone to die in peace but was fiercely insulted by those around Him. They repeated the false accusation that He wanted to destroy the temple, taunted Him to come down from the cross, mocked His ability to be anyone's Savior or King, and, in words that

---

5. This is the reading in the KJV margin. Though it could be understood as an objective genitive, i.e., a patient waiting or hope in Christ (as the KJV text reads), it seems best to read it as a subjective genitive, i.e., as the endurance that Christ Himself exercised, in parallel with the earlier phrase in 2 Thessalonians 3:5—"the love of God," that is, "God's love for us."

6. Johannes P. Louw and Eugene Albert Nida, *Greek-English Lexicon of the New Testament: Based on Semantic Domains* (New York: United Bible Societies, 1996), 307.

unwittingly fulfilled Psalm 22:8, declared, "He trusted in God; let him deliver him now." The two thieves crucified with Him hurled the same taunts and accusations at Him (see Matt. 27:39– 44). Still, as Peter observed, He did not return insult for insult or answer jeers with condemnation (see 1 Peter 2:23). He suffered silently, waiting on God and willingly laying down His life—and no doubt rejoicing that God's Word was being fulfilled!

Christ's Strength Clothed in Meekness

The meekness and gentleness of Christ are not signs of weakness, but of great inner strength, for only a mighty spiritual warrior could rule his own spirit under such provocation. Jonathan Edwards argued that in the persecuted and dying Lamb we find the highest example of Christian strength in all history:

> The directest and surest way in the world, to make a right judgment, what a holy fortitude is, in fighting with God's enemies; is to look to the captain of all God's hosts, and our great leader and example; and see wherein his fortitude and valor appeared, in his chief conflict, and in the time of the greatest battle that ever was. . . . Doubtless here we shall see the fortitude of a holy warrior and champion in the cause of God, in its highest perfection and greatest luster, and an example fit for the soldiers to follow, that fight under this captain.
>
> But how did he show his holy boldness and valor at that time? Not in the exercise of any fiery passions; not in fierce and violent speeches, and vehemently declaiming against, and crying out of the intolerable wickedness of opposers, giving 'em their own in plain terms; but in not opening his mouth when afflicted and oppressed, in going as a lamb to the slaughter, and as a sheep before his shearers, is dumb, not opening his mouth; praying that the Father would forgive his cruel enemies, because they knew not what they did; not shedding others' blood;

but with all-conquering patience and love, shedding his own. Indeed one of his disciples, that made a forward pretense to boldness for Christ, and confidently declared he would sooner die with Christ than deny him, began to lay about him with a sword: but Christ meekly rebukes him, and heals the wound he gives.

And never was the patience, meekness, love, and forgiveness of Christ, in so glorious a manifestation, as at that time. Never did he appear so much a *lamb*, and never did he show so much of the *dovelike* spirit, as at that time. If therefore we see any of the followers of Christ, in the midst of the most violent, unreasonable and wicked opposition, of God's and his own enemies, maintaining under all this temptation, the humility, quietness, and gentleness of a lamb, and the harmlessness, and love, and sweetness of a dove, we may well judge that here is a good soldier of Jesus Christ.[7]

Truly we see in Jesus Christ the fulfillment of Isaiah's prophecy. "He was oppressed, and he was afflicted, yet he opened not his mouth: he is brought as a lamb to the slaughter, and as a sheep before her shearers is dumb, so he openeth not his mouth" (Isa. 53:7). Behold the suffering Servant of Jehovah! Behold the Lamb of God, who takes away the sin of the world! If you would follow Him, then by His grace you too must learn to be both a servant and a lamb, suffering criticism quietly in submission to God.

THE ROAR OF THE LION

The words spoken by Christ during His passion reveal that He did not suffer as a victim, but as a victor. It is not our purpose

---

7. Edwards, *Religious Affections*, in *Works*, 2:350–51. Paragraph breaks have been added to assist the reader.

here to review everything that Christ said during the final hours of his life, but only to examine particular sayings relevant to how He responded to His enemies. As we noted earlier, Christ's suffering is unique in that He died as a sacrifice to atone for our sins, but Christ's suffering is also a model for what it means to endure injustice by faith. Although Christ was amazingly quiet through His ordeal, He did speak at key points, and His words teach us about how we must speak when we face criticism.

Christ Boldly Gave Himself

When Judas arrived at the garden of Gethsemane with a cohort of soldiers,[8] Jesus did not hide but walked out to meet them, asking whom they sought—though He already knew the answer. When they said "Jesus of Nazareth," Christ gave them a short answer that carried such force that these hardened military men stumbled backward and fell down on the ground. What was His reply? Literally, He said, "I am" (John 18:5). Jesus declared Himself to be the eternal *I AM*, the Lord God "which is, and which was, and which is to come, the Almighty" (Rev. 1:8; see also Ex. 3:14; John 8:58). For a moment, the glory of His divine nature broke out and rendered His enemies helpless. The crowd had come to seize a fleeing peasant, but instead encountered *fearless majesty*.[9] These wicked men could not compel the Lord of glory to go with them, much less to die on the cross. Christ was voluntarily laying down His own life, just as He said He would do, before taking it up again (see John 10:18).

When we face malicious criticism from powerful opponents,

---

8. The Greek word corresponds to a Roman cohort, ordinarily consisting of six hundred men, but it might refer here to a portion of a cohort sent for this particular task. Leon Morris, *The Gospel according to John*, The New International Commentary on the New Testament (1971; repr., Grand Rapids: Eerdmans, 1992), 741.

9. Morris, 743–44.

we can do so in the strength of knowing who Christ is and who we are in Christ. Though the world may demonize us as wrong-doers or devalue us as persons, our Lord is the great *I AM*, and we are members of His body, the church. No one can harm us, not even with their words, unless it is the will of our loving Savior. Even if we should die as martyrs, in Christ we are not mere victims, but always "more than conquerors" (Rom. 8:37).

After the soldiers recovered from this brief outburst of divine glory, Jesus again identified Himself, and said, "If therefore ye seek me, let these go their way" (John 18:8). He sought to protect His disciples from the severe trials He was about to undergo, for He would not lose any of those whom the Father had given Him. Peter had his own ideas about how to deal with the situation, and brandishing a sword, cut off the ear of the high priest's servant. Christ, however, commanded Peter to sheathe his sword and, in an amazing demonstration of love for His enemies, healed the servant's ear (see Luke 22:51; John 18:10–11).

Just when we would expect Christ to be consumed with fear and concern for His own safety, His heart overflowed with love for others. Criticism, not to mention physical danger, tends to constrict our hearts with self-centeredness. Our world shrinks down to our own troubles. We justify our selfishness by saying that life is just too hard and our emotions too raw. The Spirit of Christ, however, can enable us to break free of this crippling self-absorption. He can enlarge and empower us to give our attention and effort to the needs of others, both the loved ones under our care and even our enemies. When you are assaulted with unjust criticism, counterattack the devil by devoting yourself to loving other people. Look to Christ so that your circumstances don't control you, and instead, keep serving others in self-denying love.

When in my second charge, I was visited one evening by a schoolteacher who had sought to be accepted in the denomination as a theological student but was rejected. I knew that he was jealous of my having been accepted, but I was completely unprepared for the torrent of criticism that came out of his mouth. He told me in no uncertain terms that all my knowledge was only in my head and had not reached my heart, that I didn't know how to preach in a Reformed experiential way to comfort God's people, and that I was really a wolf in sheep's clothing—in short, that I was a hypocrite and had better seriously consider whether I should be in the ministry at all. Being overwhelmed at the time, I responded rather meekly to it all, but later that evening after he had left, this question haunted me: *What if he is right?* I wrestled for hours that night until the Lord calmed my spirit with words from Matthew 27:18 that Pilate "knew that for envy they had delivered him." Knowing that my Savior had endured on a larger scale what I was going through on a small scale, and that He endured His terrible trials and abandonments sinlessly, provided me with the grace I needed to rest in peace. The next day I was enabled by God's grace to speak with love to the schoolteachers of our denomination—with my critic sitting among them—and to interact with him graciously later that day. Happily, he called a few years later to ask forgiveness for criticizing me in the manner he had.

Christ Boldly Exposed Injustice

For all His lamblike quietness, the Lord Jesus still took time to rebuke His enemies for the wickedness of their actions. He said to His captors, "Be ye come out, as against a thief, with swords and staves? When I was daily with you in the temple, ye stretched forth no hands against me: but this is your hour, and the power of darkness" (Luke 22:52–53). If Jesus had committed a crime, then why didn't they arrest Him when He was publicly teaching in the temple courts? The very timing of His arrest showed the injustice of their case and proved that they acted under the influence of the powers of darkness. As Philip Ryken writes, "In cowardly secret they came in the dead of the night."[10]

Later when the high priest interrogated Him about His teaching, Christ said that His teaching was publicly known and easily verified, if they really cared to know the truth. Christ was appealing to an ancient Jewish principle of justice that an accused man did not have to prove his own innocence before a court, but rather his guilt must be established by the testimony of witnesses.[11] When an officer struck Jesus for answering the high priest in this manner, Jesus protested, saying, "If I have spoken evil, bear witness of the evil: but if well, why smitest thou me?" (John 18:19–23). Again, Christ was calling for justice in their handling of Him, and by so doing, underscored the injustice of their proceedings.

A quiet and meek spirit does not prevent us from speaking out against injustice. Though we must not rail and rage against accusers, and often must quietly endure criticism, at times we ought to speak up against unjust acts and illegal procedures. As God's servants, we must call people to account for their actions, press their consciences with the truth so that they might be convicted of their sins and brought to repentance, and seek to establish social and legal precedents that will protect other people from similar injustice. We should do so not out of personal vindictiveness, nor because we love our lives more than our calling, but out of a love for God and a concern for our fellow human beings. The apostle Paul confronted civil magistrates over unjust judicial procedures (see Acts 16:35–39) and asserted his legal rights when arrested (see Acts 22:24–26). This is no contradiction to Christlikeness,

10. Philip G. Ryken, *Luke*, vol. 2, *Chapters 13–24*, Reformed Expository Commentary (Phillipsburg, NJ: P&R, 2009), 519.

11. Morris, *Gospel according to John*, 755–56; George R. Beasley-Murray, *John*, Word Biblical Commentary 36, 2nd ed. (Nashville: Thomas Nelson, 1999), 324–25.

but an expression of the very heart of Jesus, who came to bring justice to the nations (see Isa. 42:1).

Christ Boldly Declared His Majesty

Christ also "witnessed a good confession" of His true identity before His persecutors. When the high priest asked Him if He was the Christ, the Son of God, Jesus said, "I am: and ye shall see the Son of man sitting on the right hand of power, and coming in the clouds of heaven" (Mark 14:62). His confession at this point in His life displays the paradox of the gospel, for from a human perspective Christ is "overpowered and cannot save himself," yet precisely here He declares that as the incarnate Son of God and the Lord's Anointed, He "reigns supreme."[12] Before Pontius Pilate, Christ professed to be the King of a spiritual kingdom that advances not by force of arms but by force of truth (see John 18:33–37).

Following in our Master's footsteps, we must never allow criticism to silence our confession of Jesus Christ (see 1 Tim. 6:12–14). The world tries to intimidate us into abandoning our witness, but we overcome the world and the devil "by the blood of the Lamb, and by the word of [our] testimony" (Rev. 12:11). Though we must quietly bear with hateful slander against our own persons, we must boldly bear witness to Christ before the world. We must assert the supreme Lordship of Jesus Christ even in the times of our greatest weakness, as He did in His.

Christ Boldly Prayed to His Father

Christ's seven sayings from the cross are well known, and this is not the place for a thorough exposition of them. It is worth

---

12. Walter W. Wessel and Mark L. Strauss, "Mark," in *The Expositor's Bible Commentary*, rev. ed., Tremper Longman III and David E. Garland (Grand Rapids: Zondervan, 2010), 9:959.

noting, however, that while the mocking crowds shouted many angry words at Jesus, the gospels do not record any retort from the dying Christ. Instead, Christ spoke words of comfort and love to His mother (see John 19:26–27) and to the repentant thief (see Luke 23:43), and expressed His own distress and triumphant hope (see John 19:28, 30). He also prayed to His Father to forgive His enemies (see Luke 23:34), which expressed His mercy to sinners. Taking up the words of the Psalms (see Mark 15:34; Luke 23:46),[13] He cried out to His Father, displaying His unwavering trust in God in the darkest hour, when God, whose "wrath is worse than all deaths," made Him who knew no sin to be sin for us (see 2 Cor. 5:21).[14] Calvin notes that "though he was fiercely attacked by violent temptations, still his faith was unshaken."[15] The weight of His sorrows could press nothing out of His holy soul except faith in His God and love for His neighbor.

When we suffer from unjust criticism and attacks against our persons, we do well to imitate Christ by devoting ourselves to prayer. Such prayers need not be eloquent. Christ's recorded prayers from the cross are remarkably brief and simple—fitting for a man dying in deep distress. His prayers also commend to us praying the Psalms. The Psalms present us with the full anatomy

---

13. Psalms 22:1; 31:5.

14. Calvin, *Commentary on a Harmony of the Evangelists*, 3:319 (exposition of Matt. 27:46). Calvin wrote, "In order that Christ might satisfy for us, it was necessary that he should be placed as a guilty person at the judgment-seat of God. Now nothing is more dreadful than to feel that God, whose wrath is worse than all deaths, is the Judge. When this temptation was presented to Christ, as if, having God opposed to him, he were already devoted to destruction, he was seized with horror. . . . No one who considers that Christ undertook the office of Mediator on the condition of suffering our condemnation, both in his body and in his soul, will think it strange that he maintained a struggle with the sorrows of death, as if an offended God had thrown him into a whirlpool of afflictions."

15. Calvin, 3:321–23 (exposition of Matt. 27:50).

of Christian experience, as Calvin observed.[16] The Psalms are, like Christ, good for both body and soul, for sufferings outward or physical, as well as sufferings inward and spiritual. Through the Spirit-given words of the psalmists, we learn to cry out to God from the depths, to lament, "How long, O LORD?" (Ps. 13:1, 2) and at the same time, to go on trusting in God and rejoicing in His salvation (see Ps. 13:5, 6). The Psalms put our suffering in a larger, God-centered, redemptive-historical perspective that gives hope and strength to believers. Even Psalm 22, which begins with the heart-wrenching cry of dereliction, "My God, my God, why hast thou forsaken me?" concludes with the assured expectation that through the exaltation of God's Afflicted One, the kingdom of God will rise and grow, gathering in worshipers from all nations. Pray and sing the psalms, and God will turn your pain under criticism into praise. "Wait on the LORD: be of good courage, and he shall strengthen thine heart: wait, I say, on the LORD" (Ps. 27:14).

After watching Jesus suffer so horrifically and seeing how He responded, the centurion was moved to say, "Truly this man was the Son of God" (Mark 15:39). If people were to closely observe your responses to unfair and harsh criticism, would they say, "Surely, this is a child of God?" We all stumble in many ways, but true godliness will show itself in how we respond to criticism, especially in how we speak to our critics and to our God. Let us walk in the footsteps of the crucified Messiah, trusting in the Father as He did, and lean on His Spirit so that His death and life may be exhibited in us for the watching world to see.

---

16. John Calvin, *Commentary on the Book of Psalms,* trans. James Anderson (Grand Rapids: Eerdmans, 1948), 1:xxxvii.

PART 2

*PRACTICAL PRINCIPLES FOR
COPING WITH CRITICISM*

3

RECEIVE CRITICISM
REALISTICALLY

Coping with criticism in the ministry requires a healthy reckoning with reality. Perhaps this strikes you as a strange point for us to make at the beginning of a section on practical principles for handling criticism. What does reality have to do with properly receiving verbal critique?

There is an unbiblical idealism that pastors can imbibe. Romanticizing the ministry, we may think that so long as we are faithful, we will not be subject to criticism. Idyllic images of a congregation overwhelmingly supportive and positively receptive of their pastor fill our minds. Is this not the way it ought to be? Or, as is probably more often the case, our high-minded self-perception can lead us to subconsciously think that we are beyond the bounds of just criticism. Many pastors with such idealistic perspectives are crushed by the unglamorous gripes of others.

There is, however, an equally dangerous perspective. It is the negativity of pessimism. While equally dangerous, pessimism is also equally unrealistic. It views criticism as a necessary evil, something that the pastor must grit his teeth and bear. There is nothing good in the criticism and nothing good that could possibly come out of it. Criticism is a threat, and so too is the critic. How quickly we can villainize our critics, painting them with a black brush. Another form of pessimism is also possible: that of an overly negative self-image. This can cause the slightest criticism to drive us to despair.

We often think of idealism and pessimism as polar opposites, but in certain ways, they are remarkably similar. They are both rejections of reality. Both flow from an unrealistic view of the ministry, ourselves, and the criticism we receive. Thus, we often find ourselves oscillating between one and the other. When our experience does not align with our idealistic expectations, we gravitate toward pessimism, and vice versa. The end result can be utter disillusionment concerning the ministry.

If we are to cope with criticism in the ministry, we must put away these unrealities. We must receive criticism realistically. But how?

REALISM ABOUT THE INEVITABILITY OF CRITICISM

First, we must be realistic about the fact that critical words, both constructive and destructive, helpful and unhelpful, come with the territory of the ministry. To say that criticism is inevitable for pastors is not overly pessimistic, but simply squares with reality. There has never been a minister or a ministry that has not been the target of verbal flak. Reckoning with this is an important first step in dealing with it when it comes our way.

As the saying goes, "To avoid criticism, do nothing, say nothing, be nothing."[1] Gospel ministry could be summed up in doing, saying, and being, all in a peculiarly public manner. The pastor

---

1. Elbert Hubbard, *Little Journeys to the Homes of American Statesmen* (New York: G. P. Putnam's Sons, 1898), 370.

carries out his various tasks, whether in administration, supervision, or visitation, all before the eyes of his congregation. He is constantly speaking truth to his people, whether through public pulpit proclamation or private instruction and counseling. Add to this the sober fact that he is called by God to be exemplary in holiness, beckoning his people to follow him as he follows Christ.

It is not merely the public nature of his doing, saying, and being that makes criticism inevitable for the pastor. Rather, verbal critique is unavoidable because of the tragic reality of sin, the destructive schemes of Satan, and the sanctifying purposes of God.

The Tragic Reality of Sin

The reality is that we as ministers are sinners. In our doing, saying, and being, we often fail to love God and our people as we ought. "In many things we offend all" (James 3:2). We are prone to selfishness, seeking our own cause and comfort. We might be rigorous in our pursuit of Christlikeness, but given our inescapable imperfection, the public nature of our station, and the unwavering qualifications of holiness required by God for ministers, we can expect to be criticized for our lack of devotion to the Lord and His people. In fact, when we are honest, we realize that our critics do not bring us low enough. Spurgeon remarks, "Brother, if any man thinks ill of you, do not be angry with him; for you are worse than he thinks you to be. If he charges you falsely on some point, yet be satisfied, for if he knew you better he might change the accusation, and you would be no gainer by the correction. If you have your moral portrait painted and it is ugly, be satisfied; for it only needs a few blacker touches and it would be still nearer the truth."[2]

2. Charles H. Spurgeon, "David Dancing before the Ark Because of His Election," *The Metropolitan Tabernacle Pulpit*, vol. 34 (Pasadena, TX: Pilgrim

I learned this rather poignantly on one memorable occasion in the ministry about thirty years ago. An elder in a church who strongly opposed my preaching began to spread a false, severely damaging rumor about me. The rumor spread throughout our denominational churches like feathers flying everywhere from a pillow ripped open. I began to pace back and forth in my study, trying to pray but unable to. I was angry and bitter, full of angst. Not knowing what to do, I grabbed a book from a shelf, flipped it open, and began to read. I hadn't read more than a page or two before the author said something like this: *If you have ever felt angry when a false rumor was spread about you by a critic, stop and consider: you really ought to be praising God that your enemy doesn't know how bad you really are. In fact, the rumor is not as bad as who you are in the depths of your heart.* I wish I could say that this wake-up call calmed my heart entirely, but I can say it took the bulk of the angst away, and I was able to be more submissive to God and go on with my work.

Add to our sinfulness our weaknesses, which may not be inherently sinful, and you have a recipe for criticism. While some men have an exceptional giftedness across a broad range of pastoral duties, none is exempt from weakness of one kind or another. Every minister will be deficient in some areas. The pastor gifted in counseling may not be the most precise theologian. The pastor especially skilled in preaching may struggle with interpersonal relationships. In God's wisdom, every under-shepherd of Christ's flock possesses weakness. And such, together with our sin, will become the object of critical words.

Criticism, however, not only evidences our sinfulness and

Publications, 1970), 361. Charles Simeon said similarly, "My enemy, whatever evil he says of me, does not reduce me so low as he would if he knew all concerning me that God does." Cited in Derek J. Prime and Alistair Begg, *On Being a Pastor: Understanding Our Calling and Work* (Chicago: Moody, 2004), 278.

weakness, but may also be a symptom of our faithfulness. How? Ultimately, because of sin—not in us but in the church and the world. Be assured that sinful flesh will express hostility toward a ministry ordered by the Word of God and empowered by the Spirit of God. John Wesley once questioned in his journal whether he was truly right with God since he had received no criticism for the entire day! If you proclaim the whole counsel of God as you should, you are bound to become a target of criticism because the truths you declare are offensive to fallen humanity. Don't be surprised, therefore, when people speak against you.

I will never forget a visit with Ernie Riesinger, a veteran pastor of considerable wisdom, who asked me a few years after I was settled in one of my pastorates, "How are things going for you?" I replied, "I really don't know, brother. It seems like people either hate me or love me." With a strong slap on my knee, he said, "That's great! It means you're getting through to your sheep. If you're getting through to them, few will feel neutral toward you. They'll either reject your message, or testify that it feeds their souls."

The Destructive Schemes of Satan

The Serpent, being God's first critic, continues his deceptive work in this present evil age. His strategy for the destruction of God's people has not changed—he lays siege to the Word of God. Satan is a pragmatist, doing whatever works to advance his cause against God. How does he try to subvert or sabotage the veracity and vitality of God's Word? Often by undermining the men commissioned and devoted to its proclamation. Calvin explains, "This is the craftiness of Satan, to draw away the hearts of men from ministers, that instruction may gradually fall into contempt. Thus not only is wrong done to innocent persons, in having their reputation unjustly wounded, (which is exceedingly base in regard to those who hold so honourable a rank,) but the authority of the sacred doctrine of God is diminished."[3] If he can undermine the messenger, he fancies he can undermine the message. When God's people have a critical heart toward their minister, they will have a closed heart to the proclamation of the Word. This is a devastating consequence of a critical spirit in the church, and Satan knows it.

Those of us who are office-bearers in the church are special objects of Satan's attention because of our past usefulness and our potential value for the cause of Christ. Ministers are among Satan's primary targets; Satan has declared war against us. He will use every weapon in his arsenal to destroy our ministries and to discredit the gospel of Jesus Christ. As Calvin says, the ministry "is not an easy and indulgent exercise, but a hard and severe warfare, where Satan is exerting all his power against us, and moving every stone for our disturbance."[4] Richard Baxter is even stronger: "Satan knows what a rout he can make of the troops if he can make the leader fall before their eyes. If Satan can ensnare your feet, your hands, your tongue, and make you fall, your troops will scatter."[5]

Satan attacks us at our weakest points—often through criticism. Like a good fisherman, he baits his hook according to our appetites. Once, on a fishing trip with my son, I was pleasantly surprised to pull in a good-sized walleye in the first five minutes. Later, several experienced fishermen told me that I shouldn't have caught that fish with "only a worm." It wasn't the right bait, but the fish was an easy catch. Far too often, we are spiritually like my walleye—easy catches, even with unsuitable bait.

3. John Calvin, *Commentaries on the Epistles to Timothy, Titus, and Philemon,* trans. William Pringle (Grand Rapids, Eerdmans, 1948), 140–41 (exposition of 1 Tim. 5:19).

4. John Calvin, *Commentary on the Gospel according to John,* trans. William Pringle (Grand Rapids: Eerdmans, 1949), 2:288 (exposition of John 21:15).

5. Richard Baxter, *The Reformed Pastor* (Edinburgh: Banner of Truth, 2001), 74–75.

Satan is aware of the fact that criticism is a powerful means to drive men from the ministry. Such verbal hostility is one of the primary reasons ministers resign. We cannot be unaware of the tactics of our spiritual foe. He will wield criticism in every form possible to lead us to throw in the towel and abandon our God-ordained post. Or at the very least, he will use criticism to harden our hearts against God's people or against our high calling.

The Sanctifying Purposes of God

Is criticism inevitable merely because of sin and Satan, however? Ministers can be tempted to perceive the inescapable reality of verbal critique in a wholly negative light. But the Lord of light is reigning over all this darkness. As pastors, we not only can expect criticism—we need it! Imagine if we pastors *never* received criticism. Would we be growing in humility, in sanctification, in Christlikeness, or would we be growing in pride, in self-sufficiency, and in self-righteousness? For those of us who know even a little of our naturally proud hearts, that is a rhetorical question!

The very God who called us into the ministry is intent on making us more faithful and fruitful in the ministry, and one of the means He uses toward that end is criticism. Whether the critique leveled against you is just or unjust, constructive or destructive, fact or fiction, you can be sure that God is ruling over it and working in it toward your conformity to Jesus Christ for His glory (see Rom. 8:28–29). In future chapters we will examine the implications of God's grace in and through criticism. For now, be encouraged by the fact that the ultimate reason criticism is inevitable for you is altogether positive! Your holy Lord wants your life and ministry to be adorned with the beauty of holiness.

We need a healthy dose of realism regarding the inevitability of criticism in the ministry. Perhaps you do not currently find yourself under the hammer of verbal critique. Praise God for a season of tranquility! But know that criticism will come, sooner or later. Sin will produce it, Satan will provoke it, and God will employ it for His purposes. Therefore, don't be surprised when it comes.

REALISM ABOUT THE SOURCE OF THE CRITICISM

There is more to receiving criticism realistically than just reckoning with its inevitability, however. Once the inevitable comes to pass, we must exercise a biblical realism concerning the source of the criticism. Again, the temptation to optimism or pessimism is a real threat here. Those with a more tender conscience may automatically assume their critic to be a prophet delivering the very rebuke of the Lord. Whereas the more pessimistic pastor, probably representative of most of us, will see his critic as an enemy seeking to undermine his ministry. The reality is that either of these could be true, but we must seek to understand the source before jumping to conclusions. A healthy dose of realism in the face of criticism will take into account who the verbal flak is coming from.

The Character of the Critic

While you should take every critic seriously, still ask yourself, What is the spiritual condition and character of my critic?

Is your critic a believer or an unbeliever? Jesus was shockingly realistic when He sent His disciples out into an unbelieving world: "I send you forth as sheep in the midst of wolves. . . . Ye shall be hated of all men for my name's sake" (Matt. 10:16, 22). We should expect to be despised by the world, and this will certainly lead to hateful speech and verbal affronts. While critique from the lips of an unbeliever may be legitimate and truthful, ordinarily it ought not to carry the weight that the criticism of a professing Christian does. This is why the psalmist says, "Let the righteous smite me; it shall be a kindness: and let him reprove me; it shall be an excellent oil, which shall not break my head" (Ps. 141:5). The antithesis between the unbeliever's native hostility toward Christ and the believer's Spirit-wrought love for Christ ought to be a large factor in considering criticism realistically.

If the criticism is coming from a Christian, what is the critic's maturity level? A criticism leveled at us that our preaching is not practical enough will be received differently depending on the source. If it comes from a relatively new believer who has little appetite for doctrine and scant understanding of its practical relevance, then your response probably ought to be to help this young Christian come to see the significance of biblical truth for life, rather than to change your preaching. If, however, it comes from a mature believer in the congregation who has a hearty appetite for the Word, then it is probably time to pause and examine yourself. Perhaps your preaching has become overly intellectual or abstract, failing to bring the grand truths of God to bear on the earthly, ordinary lives of your people.

If the criticism is coming from within the church, is it from a member who is actively involved in the church's ministry or a member on the sidelines? James Taylor writes, "Those who criticize are usually those on the fringe, who stand back and are deaf to every appeal for service."[6] Criticisms from such persons often do not merit change. This is not meant to assert that we should disregard the comments of all fringe members. Much of real value can be learned from such people, and there is often a very telling reason that they stay on the fringes; many have been badly burned. In general, we ought to seek them out and hear their

---

6. James Taylor, *Pastors under Pressure: Conflicts on the Outside, Conflicts Within* (Epsom, UK: Day One, 2001), 30.

concerns with great interest. But if the critic is an office-bearer or active member who is usually supportive, you should consider the criticism far more seriously, as you'll often find some truth in it that calls for change.

The Relationship to the Critic

When considering the source of criticism, we should also consider our relationship to the critic. Generally, the closer the critic is to us, the more serious we should consider their critique. In our internet age, it is possible for people who have never met us to criticize us, and to do so rather flippantly and thoughtlessly. How easy it is to attempt to verbally assassinate someone whom you have no relationship with. It is also far easier to misunderstand or misrepresent someone whom we do not know personally. Thus, criticism from those who possess little to no relationship with us should be considered with a grain of salt. Verbal flak from a first-time visitor at your church or an anonymous commenter on social media carries little weight or *gravitas*.

But if the critique comes from a close friend, family member, or colleague, it is time for us to pay attention. This is especially the case if the critic has championed or at least supported our ministry up to this point. How close are you to the critic? How intimately does he or she know you? And how supportive has your critic been of your ministerial pursuits? Answering these questions will promote realism in your perception of the criticism and your reception of it.

The Number of Critics

Along with this, we need to ask how pervasive the criticism is. Is it coming from a single person? Or is the extent of this criticism broader, coming from many different people? "Solitary shots should be ignored," writes Marshall Shelley, "but when they come from several directions, it's time to pay attention."[7] It is an overstatement to say we should ignore solitary criticisms, especially if coming from one of our sheep. But the point is well taken. The more extensive the criticism, the more attention we should give to it. Determining its extent will help us to respond realistically.

We can easily overreact to complaints that are raised by a few. There is, of course, a difference between a complaint being raised by three people in a congregation of fifteen and by three people in a congregation of one thousand. In a large congregation, a change made for a few will often provoke more people than the change satisfies. In my first charge, I learned this the hard way. When three women came to the elders to complain about one of the women's groups in the church, the elders voted to change it, only to have fifteen women come to the next meeting to complain about the change that the elders had made!

REALISM ABOUT WHAT LIES BEHIND THE CRITICISM

Intimately connected to the source of the criticism is the reason behind it. What are the person's motivations or intentions in dishing out this verbal barrage? And especially in cases where the criticism is unjust, what struggles in this person's life might lead him or her to attack you in this way?

The Motives of the Critic

Motives are a tricky thing. Even the most sanctified Christian does not possess pure motives. Our intentions are always plagued with self-serving pride. If we would receive criticism realistically, we should seek to identify the *chief* motive of our critics. Are they

---

7. Marshall Shelley, *Well-Intentioned Dragons: Ministering to Problem People in the Church* (Carol Stream, IL: Christianity Today, 1985), 110.

ultimately seeking our good and the good of our ministry? Or are they seeking to discourage and destroy? As a general rule, give your critic the benefit of the doubt; assume that his or her principal motivation is good, unless you have solid grounds to think otherwise.

Motives can often be discerned simply by the character of the critic and the relationship you have to the critic. If verbal critique is coming from a godly man who is a close friend, then ordinarily he will be criticizing you with intentions of betterment. But even if you know relatively little about your critic, it is possible to discern heart motivations by the criticism itself. If it is fueled by anger, structured around half-truths, and terminated with no hope for change, then it is quite obvious what the underlying motives are.

To be clear, right motives are no guarantee that the criticism itself is right. It may be dead wrong. But where good intentions are discerned, we should generally be more open to the critique. Those who evidence a genuine desire to strengthen our ministry should have our ear.

The Struggles of the Critic

The evidence of evil motives, however, is no excuse to shut down. The tendency when we are under the fires of unwarranted criticism is to focus on ourselves. We can fall prey to a scrupulous introspection or wallow in self-pity. The gospel, however, calls us to esteem or value our critics above ourselves (see Phil. 2:4–5). When being verbally attacked, we need to recognize that our critic is a person just like us with struggles similar to our own.

Often destructive criticism tells us less about us and more about our critic.[8] It may be symptomatic of a deeper sickness or

---

8. Leith Anderson, *How to Act Like a Christian* (Nashville: Abingdon Press, 2006), 75.

distress in his or her life. Unresolved anger, depression, changes in life, frustration in relationships, jealousy, shattered expectations, and dissatisfaction with work can all be roots of criticism. When we encounter such verbal flak, we should ask, "What is happening in this person's life that would lead him or her to say these hurtful and untrue things?"

James Denney perceptively asserts, "The natural man loves to find fault; it gives him at the cheapest rate the comfortable feeling of superiority."[9] This is often true of our ill-willed critics. Faultfinding may divert attention from their guilty consciences or their broken marriages or their dire financial situations. Faultfinding may feed their autonomous dislike of the God-given authority of their elders and pastors. Faultfinding may be how they cope with their own insecurities and fears.[10] Whatever may be the case, destructive criticism is always symptomatic of a deeper issue in the critic. And if we would receive it realistically, we need to discern what that deeper issue is.

OPEN YOUR EYES

Nothing is easier than having faulty perceptions of ourselves, our ministry, and our critics. But if we would honor God and persevere under criticism, we cannot live in this fictional world of unrealities. We need to open our eyes. We need to own the inevitability of criticism. We need to admit our sins and weaknesses for what they are. We need to reckon with where criticism is coming from and why. Most of all, we need to see a gracious God using every critique to accomplish His eternal purpose of making us like Christ.

9. Quoted in James Taylor, *Pastors under Pressure*, 30–31.
10. Daniel E. Miller, *When Others Make Your Life Difficult* (Berlin, OH: TSG International, 2014), 43.

4

RECEIVE CRITICISM HUMBLY

"What three graces does a minister need most?" Many answers could be given to this question, but perhaps none rivals the wisdom of Augustine. "Humility; humility; humility," he said.[1] As pastors, we stand in desperate need of the grace of humility. This is especially so given the fact that we will be a prime target of verbal critique.

HUMBLE YOURSELF BEFORE YOUR GOD

Few things expose our hearts like criticism. When our character, reputation, abilities, or work are being questioned or denigrated, the state of our heart is immediately laid bare. This is one reason why criticism is a gracious gift from God. It exposes how self-centered we really are.

The Enemy of Humility

We are by nature prideful. The self is the center of our universe. C. S. Lewis wisely noted that pride is fueled by "the

---

1. See Augustine, "Letters of St. Augustin," in *Nicene and Post-Nicene Fathers*, ed. Philip Schaff (Grand Rapids: Eerdmans, 1994), 1:445–46.

pleasure of being above the rest."[2] It is a form of self-deification. The tragedy of all sin is that it turns us from God; the double tragedy of pride is that it turns us against God in an attempt to lift self above God. It opposes and defies His very being and sovereignty. Vaunting itself as God, it seeks to dethrone the Lord of hosts, to un-god God and to put self on the throne. Pride is anti-god, and it naturally accompanies us from birth to death. No parent has ever had to teach his or her child how to be proud. In our covenant head Adam, we fell from what we were through proud desire to be what we were not. As George Swinnock said, "Pride is the shirt of the soul, put on first [in paradise] and put off last [in death.]"[3] By nature, we puff ourselves up with false notions of self-importance and self-satisfaction, doing everything in our power to serve and preserve this fatally skewed perception of who we really are.

Pride is not satisfied, however, with its own high estimation, but wants all the world to join in praising and adoring the self. In our arrogance, we desire others to affirm that we really are as great as we have deceived ourselves into believing we are. Again, Lewis writes, "The pleasure of pride is like the pleasure of scratching. If there is an itch one does want to scratch; but it is much nicer to have neither the itch nor the scratch. As long as we have the itch of self-regard we shall want the pleasure of self-approval."[4] The itches of self-regard, self-importance, and self-entitlement provoke the need for the scratches of self-promotion and self-praise. Thus, in our high estimation of self we find great pleasure in the approval and commendation of others. It scratches us right where we itch. But, as you have surely experienced, the scratch of man's

2. C. S. Lewis, *Mere Christianity* (New York: HarperCollins, 1980), 122.

3. I. D. E. Thomas, comp., *The Golden Treasury of Puritan Quotations* (Chicago: Moody Press, 1975), 224.

4. C. S. Lewis, *Letters of C. S. Lewis,* ed. W. H. Lewis (New York: Harcout, Brace and World, 1966), 256.

approval provides only a temporary satisfaction. The itch quickly returns, causing us to crave fresh achievement and applause.

So long as we remain in the mortal body, pride clings to us—and profoundly and deeply so. Jonathan Edwards once said that pride is like an onion—if you peel off one layer, there is always another layer beneath it. And with pride comes the hankering after man's approval. The pastoral office itself, being a position of honor and authority, can easily become a snare in this regard. "Human nature can never be raised to distinction," warns Charles Bridges, "without being tempted to vanity."[5] We can subtly believe ourselves to be more holy, more wise, and more important than our people. We can operate with a sense of entitlement, thinking we deserve compliments, encouragements, and acceptance. After all, we work so hard and do so much.

Where this mentality exists, we will never be able to profit from criticism. It will either infuriate us that someone would dare attack our self-complex, or it will crush us because our self-image is founded on the praise of men. Pride will either lead us to become defensive or devastated in the face of criticism. In many cases, it will lead us to be both simultaneously. But the one thing pride will not allow us to do is receive criticism rightly.

The Fittingness of Humility

The only way to be prepared to rightly receive criticism is to cultivate an ever-deepening humility, putting to death what is earthly in us by the power of Christ's cross. We must be daily dying to our self-exalting flesh that we might live for the exaltation of Jesus Christ alone. Due to the nature of pride, we ought to be aiming and praying for Christ-appreciation and self-depreciation—even self-annihilation—so that genuine humility

5. Charles Bridges, *The Christian Ministry with an Inquiry into the Causes of Its Inefficiency* (repr., Edinburgh: Banner of Truth, 1959), 154.

would be cultivated in us and our wicked pride would be morti-
fied. Pride is not befitting of the Christian, much less the Christian minister. If we truly understand God, ourselves, and the
nature of our ministerial calling we will recognize that a humble
meekness befits us, for spiritual humility and spiritual pride are
antithetical to each other. As Stephen Charnock said, "A proud
faith is as much a contradiction as a humble devil."[6]

The main reason why we are so puffed up with self is that
we have little spiritual perception of God in His glory. As Calvin famously remarked, "man is never sufficiently touched and
affected by the awareness of his lowly state until he has compared
himself with God's majesty."[7] Low views of God promote high
views of self, whereas high views of God help us see our true
state. We would do well to meditate on God's transcendent, self-
sufficient, eternal, unchanging majesty, along with His spotless
purity, moral equity, and steadfast love and faithfulness. One
cannot believingly behold the glory of God in general and special revelation without his self-promoting pride being deflated.
"Humility," writes John Piper, "follows God like a shadow."[8]
When one has a genuine encounter with the living God, this
grace of lowliness will be present.

Such a knowledge of God is the surest way to have a proper
knowledge of ourselves. Perceiving God's infinite majesty, we
come to see our creaturely finitude and weakness. As we behold
God's thrice holy purity, we recognize the wretchedness of our
condition and the waywardness of our hearts.[9] And as we relish

6. Cited in I. D. E. Thomas, *A Puritan Golden Treasury* (Edinburgh: Banner
of Truth, 1977), 223.
7. John Calvin, *Institutes of the Christian Religion*, trans. Ford Lewis Battles,
ed. John T. McNeill (Philadelphia: Westminster Press, 1960), 1.1.3.
8. John Piper, *Future Grace* (Sisters, OR: Multnomah, 1995), 85.
9. *Overcoming Sin & Temptation,* ed. Kelly M. Kapic and Justin Taylor
(Wheaton, IL: Crossway, 2006), 283. John Owen writes, "The man that

God's incomprehensible love and grace in Christ, we acknowledge our powerlessness to redeem ourselves and our utterly hopeless condition apart from the Savior. Here is what we are by nature: finite, weak, sinful, wayward, helpless, and hopeless. Is it not unfitting for us to exalt such a self? How could a person whose heart is like yours and ours ever be proud in the presence of the holy, spotless God?[10]

Paul Tripp argues that "we're addicted to the pursuit of self-glory because, when we look in the mirror, we think we see someone who deserves to be glorified."[11] Is this true of you? Then look into the mirror of God's Word and God's glory and see yourself as you truly are by nature. Every grace and gift, including that which equips you to be a minister of the gospel, is from God. "For who maketh thee to differ from another? and what hast thou that thou didst not receive? now if thou didst receive it, why dost thou glory [i.e., boast], as if thou hadst not received it?" (1 Cor. 4:7). Self-glorification is unbefitting of those who are natively bankrupt. Every good that is ours is ours by free grace. God's grace leaves no room for self-glory; grace and pride cannot cohabit.

A prideful pastor is a contradiction in terms. The very title *minister* means *servant*—a humble Christ and a proud Christian servant have nothing to do with each other. "Forget not," writes Abraham Booth, "that the whole of your work is ministerial; not

---

understands the evil of his own heart, how vile it is, is the only useful, fruitful, and solid believing and obedient person. . . . Let us, then, consider our hearts wisely, and then go and see if we can be proud of our gifts, our graces, our valuation and esteem among professors, our enjoyments."

10. Richard Mayo, "What Must We Do to Prevent and Cure Spiritual Pride?" in *Puritan Sermons 1659–1689: The Morning Exercises at Cripplegate* (Wheaton, IL: Richard Owen Roberts, 1981), 3:390.

11. Paul David Tripp, "More Highly Than You Ought," Paul Tripp Ministries, Inc. blog, February 3, 2015, https://www.paultripp.com/articles/posts/more-highly-than-you-ought.

legislative—that you are not a lord in the church, but a servant."[12] As one who follows Christ, your God-given task as a pastor is not to be served, but to serve and to lay down your life for your flock. Such self-sacrifice is antithetical to prideful self-promotion. Is your ministry about you? Your name? Your comfort? Your glory? Or is your chief motivation to build up the church through the exaltation of Jesus Christ unto the glory of God? Christ-magnifying, servant-hearted humility alone befits the ministry.[13]

If you would be fit for the fires of criticism, you must put on meekness. To the extent that life and ministry are about you, you can be certain that critique will be poorly received and poorly benefited from.

The Blessing of Humility

When true gospel humility is present, however, one is enabled to not only receive criticism, but to be blessed by it. Even the most unjust and destructive forms of criticism can do good to the humble soul. "God resisteth the proud, and giveth grace to the humble" (1 Peter 5:5). As we saw in the previous chapter, God uses criticism as a means to conform us more to the image of Jesus Christ. When we possess a posture of humility before Him, He will give us grace to receive even the most hateful verbal flak in a way that serves His sanctifying purpose.

What a wellspring of encouragement this should be to us! When our service to God is married to a Spirit-wrought passion for the glory of God and the good of His people, then we can be

12. Abraham Booth, "Pastoral Cautions," in *The Christian Pastor's Manual,* ed. John Brown (repr., Pittsburgh: Soli Deo Gloria, 1990), 66.

13. *The Reformed Pastor,* ed. William Brown (repr., Edinburgh: Banner of Truth, 1974), 116. Richard Baxter warns us, "Pride is a vice that ill beseems them that must lead men in such an humble way to heaven: let us, therefore, take heed, lest, when we have brought others thither, the gate should prove too strait for ourselves."

confident of God's grace and blessing on our lives and ministries, even when men seek our demise. If the living God is for us, who can stand against us? Study the Bible and church history, and you will find that the ministries that have had the evident blessing of God on them were often fiercely assailed and opposed. No man can stop the blessing of God. And God's blessing resides with the humble. Bridges writes, "It is of little comparative moment, that our ministry should bear the stamp of talent, erudition, or pathos. But if it should be characterized by the savour of humility and love, it would be best adapted to display the glories of Immanuel, and most honoured with the manifestations of his Spirit."[14]

Do you desire to respond to criticism in a healthy way? Do you desire to truly profit from it? Do you desire the Spirit-empowered blessing of God on your ministry in the midst of it? Then, brother, clothe yourself with humility!

HUMBLE YOURSELF BEFORE YOUR CRITIC

Receiving criticism humbly may conjure up images of a weak and timid pushover who is always being taken advantage of. That is not what we are advocating. True humility exudes a certain strength and confidence. It is not the might of self-sufficiency; it is a confident strength in the sufficiency of God and His grace. The truly humble person fears God. The horizon of his vision is pervaded with the greatness of God. He also knows that by way of gracious covenant, he belongs to God. He is no longer his own. Life is no longer about him. His chief end is the glory of God. His soul's delight is in obedience to God. He values the smile of God above all else.

Such a humble, God-fearing confidence does not produce

14. Bridges, *Christian Ministry*, 154.

weaklings who are easy prey. Rather it forges men who are marked by self-control and others-oriented love. It delivers from false self-perceptions, egotistic self-defense, and vain pursuits of the praise of man. Tim Keller defines such meekness as "the freedom of self-forgetfulness." He explains, "True gospel-humility means I stop connecting every experience, every conversation, with myself. In fact, I stop thinking about myself."[15] Christlike humility liberates us from ourselves to fix our attention on God and others. In our reception of criticism, it will manifest itself in at least three ways: inclining your ear, inspecting your heart, and involving others.

Incline Your Ear

First, the gospel-humble pastor will incline his ear. He will listen carefully to his critic. This is not something that comes easy for most pastors. We are used to doing the talking. Our job consists in an unending sequence of preaching, teaching, counseling, and giving advice. As ambassadors of Christ, we are called to use our lips to proclaim the excellencies of Jesus Christ and to help His sheep understand and apply gospel truth to their own lives. But it is possible for all of this verbal ministry to be employed at the expense of the ministry of good listening. We become very good at moving our mouths, but not so good at lending our ears. Jason Helopoulos expresses this very concern: "A glaring fault in many, if not most, pastors is that they are poor listeners. In fact, I find pastors to be some of the poorest listeners I have been around."[16] Many pastors get so used to doing the talking that they forget what it means to really hear people out. And if this is true in a general sense, how much more so in the

15. Timothy Keller, *The Freedom of Self-Forgetfulness: The Path to True Christian Joy* (Leyland: 10Publishing, 2012), 32.

16. Jason Helopoulos, *The New Pastor's Handbook: Help and Encouragement for the First Years of Ministry* (Grand Rapids: Baker, 2015), 100.

face of criticism. If we do not listen to our sheep when they think highly of us, will we not be even less inclined to listen when they are critiquing us?

In our prideful self-defensiveness, we can often respond to criticism before we have taken the time to really hear and understand the critique. Proverbs 18:13 warns, "He that answereth a matter before he heareth it, it is folly and shame unto him." Are you really listening well to your critic before answering him? Failing to get the facts straight will lead to our dishonor. As pastors we need to be "swift to hear, slow to speak, slow to wrath" (James 1:19). When criticism comes, humility will evidence itself in a self-restraint that genuinely values the critic as a person and the critique itself. Deborah Riegel challenges us at this point, "If you already believe you know better than the person you're listening to, you're not listening. If you already have advice to give, you're not listening. If you already know how this story turns out, you're not listening. If you're already listening only to the parts of the story that confirm your beliefs, you're not listening. And if you already have your counterattack planned, you're not listening."[17]

Listening is not just a task for our ears, but surprisingly for our mouths. David Mathis writes, "Good listening asks perceptive, open-ended questions, that don't tee up yes-no answers, but gently peel the onion and probe beneath the surface."[18] For example, let's say a church member expresses a concern that your preaching has become legalistic.

17. Deborah Grayson Riegel, "The Crucial Body Part All Great Leaders Must Enhance," *Fast Company*, August 12, 2013, http://www.fastcompany .com/3015511/leadership-now/the-crucial-body-part-all-great-leaders -must-enhance.

18. David Mathis, "Six Lessons in Good Listening," Desiring God blog, April 3, 2014, https://www.desiringgod.org/articles/six-lessons-in-good -listening.

- When a critique is confusing or unclear, ask for clarification and definition. "Could you help me understand exactly what you mean by 'legalistic'?" "When did you begin to sense that my preaching was going in this direction?"
- When a critique is general and vague, ask for more specific examples. "Could you share a particular instance where my preaching fell into legalism?"
- When a critique presents the situation as beyond repair, ask for a solution. "How could this be fixed?" "What do you think specifically needs to change in my preaching to avoid this error?"
- When a critique is clearly not the root problem, ask questions that may bring the underlying issue to light. "Since we are talking about these things, is there anything else in my ministry or life that has concerned, offended, or hurt you?"
- When a critique is clearly erroneous, ask questions that will cause your critic to go to the Scriptures. "What would you say the Bible teaches about the relationship of the Christian to the law? Do you think obedience to God is essential to healthy Christianity?"

Along with asking questions, it may be helpful to summarize the criticism. "Let me make sure I am understanding you rightly. Are you saying . . . ?"

In all this we must consider not only the questions we are asking, but how we are asking them. There is a way to ask questions—particularly with our tone of voice and our body posture—that exudes impatience and frustration. But when graciously asked, such questions show our critics that we really care about their criticism. They also help us to get a clearer grasp of the problem and how best to respond.

Humble listening can have a soothing effect on our initially agitated critics. Pastor's wife Ruth Shaw writes, "I have found that time spent listening can diffuse a lot of tension, and that some people just want to be listened to!"[19] When critics see that we don't immediately shut down or counterattack, they often will calm down themselves. When they sense that we genuinely love them and value their critique, they will be more prone to value our response, whatever it might be. Ultimately, however, we are to listen to our critics not because of the value it brings to us, but because it magnifies our meek Savior.

Inspect Your Heart

Humility will evidence itself, second, in inspecting the heart. The humble pastor recognizes the fact that he is weak, errant, and sinful. He understands that he needs criticism. He knows that critics of every shape and size are one of the great means God uses to sanctify him and strengthen his ministry. He is, therefore, slow to respond and quick to examine himself in light of the critique.

If a member of your congregation expresses viable concerns that you are antisocial, what would such self-examination look like? Here are a few thoughts:

- *Examine your actions.*
  - "Do I spend the vast majority of my time in the study?"
  - "Do I actively engage in times of fellowship after worship services and throughout the week?"
  - "Is my home a place of regular hospitality?"
  - "Are there areas in my ministry where I am failing to love my people?"

19. Ruth Shaw, "Forgiveness and Forbearance: Handling Criticism," in *The Minister's Wife: Privileges, Pressures and Pitfalls,* ed. Ann Benton (Downers Grove, IL: InterVarsity Press, 2011), 135.

- *Examine your emphases.*
  - "Do I stress study and sermon preparation over knowing and engaging my sheep?"
  - "Is family visitation and counseling put on the back burner due to prioritizing administrative tasks or denominational responsibilities?"
  - "What would proper balance look like in these areas, and does my ministry exemplify it?"
- *Examine your tone.*
  - "When people call me, do I exude an eager warmth or an annoyed frustration?"
  - "When in meetings or counseling sessions do I show a genuine delight in others, giving them my undivided attention, or am I constantly looking at my watch?" Three decades ago, a parishioner taught me a valuable lesson in this regard. When I picked up the phone with a sigh, a voice said, "Why the big sigh, pastor? Am I that much of an interruption?" In an instant, I saw my faulty thinking: I was treating my study as if that was the most important part of my work, and I was treating my parishioner as if he was an interruption. In reality, people come first; they are not interruptions!
- *Examine your motives.*
  - "Why is it that I spend so much time alone in my study? Is it because I believe it is the best way I can serve my flock? Or is it for self-serving ends?"
  - "Do I love books more than people?"
- *Examine your personality.*
  - "How does the way God has made me play into this critique?"
  - "Does the fact that I am an introvert change, in any way, how I should receive and respond to this criticism?"

Such heart inspection typically cannot be carried out in the heat of the moment. It requires time, quiet reflection, and a measure of emotional stability. If the critique has the potential to be legitimate and true, even in part, ask the critic for a day or two to process it. "The heart of the righteous studieth to answer: but the mouth of the wicked poureth out evil things" (Prov. 15:28).

Along with examining ourselves in light of the *content* of criticism, we ought to undergo self-inspection in the *context* of criticism. How am I responding to this criticism? What is going on in my heart? Am I prayerful? Am I feeling defensive or angry? Has the criticism inflamed a critical or bitter spirit in my heart toward my critic? What am I communicating to my critic with my body language (i.e., eye contact, facial expressions, hand motions, posture, and so on)? Have I said or asked anything that has made the problem worse? We ought to ask ourselves these and so many other questions as a means of growing in our ability to humbly receive criticism.

Involve Others

Third, a humble reception of criticism will involve others. When we sense our limited understanding of the situation and our often misguided self-perceptions, we will seek the counsel of godly men and women in our life. The humble pastor is willing to expose his potential faults to mature and trusted companions.

Great care is needed here. It is important that we choose the right people to involve. Do not share the criticism with those who will tell you what you simply *want* to hear, but who will tell you what you *need* to hear. Also, ensure that the people brought into the situation are not gossips and have the ability to maintain complete confidentiality. Often your wife is the best initial person to involve when facing criticism. Our wives can be honest with us because they know us and care about us deeply. A trustworthy friend or a fellow minister or elder from another church may also prove to be of great help.

We must also take care to have right motives. Why are we involving others? Is it so that we can slander our critic? So that we can make ourselves feel better about the situation? Or is it that we might get a fresh perspective on the problem from someone who knows us well? Involving others can easily be motivated by arrogant self-promotion and lead to gossip. But the truly humble pastor will involve others to assist him in discerning to what extent the criticism is truthful.

When approaching your confidants, first, share the criticism with them. Seek to paint it with a clear and honest brush. Second, share your perspective on the criticism and what you think the best response would be. And third, ask for their insight. "Am I thinking rightly about this criticism?" "Do you think there is truth in this critique?" "Would this be the best way to respond or is there a better way?" More often than not, your confidants will have some valuable suggestions that you had not considered. Such advice is invaluable and can save many heartaches in the years of ministry ahead.

ARE YOU HUMBLE?

Perhaps no virtue is more needed when it comes to coping with criticism than humility. Jesus perfectly exemplified such a self-forgetting, others-oriented disposition (see Phil. 2:5–8), and He pronounced eternal blessedness on those who followed in His meek footsteps (see Matt. 5:5). Are you meek? Is your soul clothed in the gospel-garments of humility? Examine yourself in light of the piercing words of Martyn Lloyd-Jones:

> The meek man is not proud of himself, he does not in any sense glory in himself. He feels that there is nothing in himself of

which he can boast. . . . Then let me go further; the man who is meek is not even sensitive about himself. He is not always watching himself and his own interests. He is not always on the defensive. We all know about this, do we not? Is it not one of the greatest curses in life as a result of the fall—this sensitivity about self? We spend the whole of our lives watching ourselves. But when a man becomes meek he has finished with all that; he no longer worries about himself and what other people say. To be truly meek means we no longer protect ourselves, because we see there is nothing worth defending. So we are not on the defensive; all that is gone. The man who is truly meek never pities himself, he is never sorry for himself. He never talks to himself and says, 'You are having a hard time, how unkind these people are not to understand you.' He never thinks: 'How wonderful I really am, if only other people gave me a chance.' Self-pity! What hours and years we waste in this! But the man who has become meek has finished with all that. . . . When a man truly sees himself, he knows nobody can say anything about him that is too bad. You need not worry about what men may say or do; you know you deserve it all and more. . . . The man who is truly meek is the one who is amazed that God and man can think of him as well as they do and treat him as well as they do.[20]

Let us close this chapter with a notable example of the power and benefits of humility. Some years ago, a recalcitrant member in a sister church was proudly rebuffing the attempts of one elder after another to lead him to repent of a sinful and critical spirit that was sowing seeds of division within the church. In addition to refusing to repent, this member treated each elder who visited

20. D. Martyn Lloyd-Jones, *Studies in the Sermon on the Mount* (London: Inter-Varsity Fellowship, 1959), 1:69.

him with contempt. He was, in fact, blatantly obnoxious. The elders finally met to discuss placing this offending member under the first formal step of church discipline. During the discussion, the only elder who had not visited this member asked if he could also visit him before formal discipline was enacted, to which the elders agreed.

When the recalcitrant member began to criticize the elders and the church yet again to the final elder to visit him, this godly and humble elder stood up, walked over to the angry member, and literally lay down on the floor in front of him. From his prone position, he then said in a humble and imploring tone of voice, "Dear friend and brother, I would rather that you walk all over me than hear you speak against my brother elders or persist further in your sin. Please stand up and walk over me; make me your floor mat. I would rather that you hurt me physically than injure your own soul for eternity or disturb the church with your criticisms."

The genuine humility of this dear elder convicted this rebellious man. He broke into a flood of tears, repented of his sin on the spot, and confessed his guilt for speaking ill of the elders and for sowing seeds of discord in the body of Christ. And his repentance proved to be genuine.

Please don't misunderstand. We are not recommending that everyone should follow this same practice literally in dealing and coping with criticism, but we are advocating that we exercise, by God's grace, the same gift and spirit of humility as one primary way among others of responding to and coping with criticism.

5

RESPOND WITH
SOBER JUDGMENT

Every day in the United States approximately thirty people are killed in car crashes resulting from drunk driving.[1] Intoxication with alcohol significantly impairs one's ability to think clearly and respond quickly. And the consequences are devastating. How many tens of thousands of people would be alive today were it not for drunkenness?

A lack of sobriety has similarly devastating effects in the Christian life and ministry. It is so easy to be intoxicated with the lies of the world, the flesh, and the devil. And this temptation is only heightened in the face of criticism. If our minds are drunk with untruths or half-truths, our response to criticism could be fatal to our ministries, our souls, or our critics. This is why Peter, writing to a church suffering persecution, calls them to "gird up the loins of [their] mind" and to "be sober" (1 Peter 1:13). We need to have minds girded up with truth. We need spiritual sobriety. Such sober-mindedness will manifest itself in a prayerful, patient, and prudent response to criticism.

1. "Drunk Driving," National Highway Traffic Safety Administration, accessed July 15, 2020, https://www.nhtsa.gov/risky-driving/drunk-driving.

BE PRAYERFUL

It is possible for us to know much about God without really knowing God.[2] Pastors must be ever watchful of this danger. How do you know that your knowledge of the truth is translating into a true knowledge of God? Take a good look at your prayer life. Martyn Lloyd-Jones once said, "If your knowledge of doctrine does not make you a great man of prayer, you had better examine yourself again."[3] Elsewhere he maintained, "Those who know God best are the ones who speak to him most of all."[4] Is it possible for us to have the Word of Christ dwelling in us richly and to have minds renewed with divine wisdom and yet not be prayerful? The obvious answer is no.

The sober-minded pastor will be a praying pastor. He will understand that prayer and preaching are his two primary ministerial tasks—as Acts 6:4 states, "We will give ourselves continually to prayer, and to the ministry of the word"—and that prayer is listed first! As Charles Bridges wrote, "Prayer is one half of our ministry; and it gives to the other half all its power and success."[5] Thus, the godly pastor will strive to take hold both of himself and of God in prayer. He will take hold of himself by remembering the priority and value of prayer, by showing sincerity in his prayers, by cultivating a continual spirit of prayer, by striving for balance in his prayers, and by praying earnestly for others—including his critics! He will strive to take hold of God in prayer

2. J. I. Packer, *Knowing God* (Downers Grove, IL: InterVarsity, 1993), 18–23.

3. Quoted in Dick Alderson, comp., "The Wisdom of Martyn Lloyd-Jones: Selections of Sayings," *Banner of Truth*, no. 275 (August/September, 1986): 7.

4. D. Martyn Lloyd-Jones, *The Assurance of Our Salvation: Studies in John 17* (Wheaton, IL: Crossway, 2000), 33.

5. Charles Bridges, *The Christian Ministry with an Inquiry into the Causes of Its Insufficiency*, 3rd ed. (London: Seeley and Burnside, 1830), 193.

by returning to Him His own Word—that is, showing Him His own handwriting; by pouring his heart out to the entire Trinity in prayer, finding access to the Father through the Son and by the Spirit; and by truly believing in prayer also in reference to those who persecute him.[6]

Charles Simeon, a Reformed Anglican preacher in the late eighteenth century, faced severe opposition from his people in Cambridge, England. His students at Cambridge would regularly interrupt his worship services and even throw stones through the windows of the church. Their frustration was due to his pointed, warm-hearted, evangelical preaching. Along with students, many of his congregants made it clear that he was an unwanted pastor. The pew-holders of his church locked the pews so that people were forced to stand in the aisles during worship services. They did this, not for one week, but for more than ten years! After a week of such treatment, most of us would be putting out our resumes in search of a new place of ministry. But what is astounding about Simeon is that he stayed for fifty-four years! He devoted his life to this hostile congregation, sacrificially loving them and zealously proclaiming the whole counsel of God to them.

What explains Simeon's perseverance? He was a man who knew his God. It was said of him that he woke up every day at four o'clock in the morning to spend the first four hours of his day in prayer and the devotional reading of the Word.[7] He had a sober mind. And thus, when asked by a friend how he withstood persecution from his own flock for so many years, Simeon responded, "My dear brother, we must not mind a little suffering for Christ's sake."[8]

6. For an expansion of this paragraph into a chapter, see Joel R. Beeke, "Prayerful Praying Today," in *Taking Hold of God,* ed. Joel R. Beeke and Brian Najapfour (Grand Rapids: Reformation Heritage Books, 2011), 223–40.

7. H. C. G. Moule, *Charles Simeon* (London: InterVarsity, 1948), 66.

8. Quoted in John Piper, *21 Servants of Sovereign Joy: Faithful, Flawed, and*

Examples like this have long assisted me in coping with criticism. For decades I have kept this helpful quotation from Charles Spurgeon taped to my computer screen where I can read it every day: "Overcome the world by patiently enduring all the persecution that falls to your lot. Do not get angry; and do not become downhearted. Jests break no bones; and if you had any bone broken for Christ's sake, it would be the most honored bone in your whole body."[9]

As we saw with Moses, Nehemiah, and Christ, our response to criticism must begin, not horizontally, but vertically. Biblical sobriety calls us to reckon first with God, then our fellow man. If we would reply to criticism in a manner that honors the Lord, we must be well-acquainted with the secret place, which assists us in making God big and people small in our personal estimation.[10]

Prayer's Perspective

Prayer is the bowing of the soul in willing submission to God. If we know God and ourselves, this posture of submissive surrender will be our reflex response when hit with criticism. We will get low before God, acknowledging our creatureliness, sinfulness, and neediness. We will cry out to Him for grace and help in our time of need, knowing that He alone has the resources needed to walk through this fiery trial.

The story is told of a friend who approached Alexander Whyte, an able Scottish preacher, with some bad news. He told Whyte that a preacher who had come to town was severely criticizing one of Whyte's colleagues. Whyte immediately responded

---

Fruitful (Wheaton, IL: Crossway, 2018), 319.

9. Charles Spurgeon, *The Metropolitan Tabernacle Pulpit* (Pasadena, TX: Pilgrim Publications, 1977), 47:593.

10. Edward T. Welch, *When People Are Big and God Is Small: Overcoming Peer Pressure, Codependency, and the Fear of Man* (Phillipsburg, NJ: P&R, 1997).

with righteous anger, stating that such criticism was unjustified, sinful, and wrong. Then the friend said that he felt compelled to bring more bad news, telling Whyte that the preacher in town was also criticizing Whyte severely. In response, Whyte showed no anger, but simply asked to be excused for a few minutes. A bit later he returned to his friend and said with great humility, "By God's grace, may the critic not be right." The friend said it was obvious that Whyte took the criticism straight to the Lord in prayer, which profoundly impacted his entire demeanor for good.

True prayer is perspective altering. "When prayer rises to its true level," writes David McIntyre, "self, with its concerns and needs, is for the time forgotten, and the interests of Christ fill, and sometimes overwhelm, the soul."[11] Is not much of our restlessness in the face of criticism the result of an obsessive fixation on ourselves? Prayer reorients our focus away from self and toward Christ. In so doing, it provides clarity of mind and warmth of soul, decreases our anxiety level, and rekindles our passion for what is right and true.

After Lot parted from Abram, God told the patriarch, "Lift up now thine eyes, and look from the place where thou art northward, and southward, and eastward, and westward" (Gen. 13:14). Abram needed this large perspective to refresh his faith and remember that God was still in charge. Jonathan Edwards once wrote, "While [Christians] are praying, he gives them sweet views of his glorious grace, purity, sufficiency, and sovereignty; and enables them with great quietness, to rest in him, to leave themselves and their prayers with him, submitting to his will, and trusting in his grace and faithfulness."[12] We need such "sweet views" of God's majesty and the greater prospects of the

11. David McIntyre, *The Hidden Life of Prayer: The Life-Blood of the Christian* (Ross-shire: Christian Focus, 2010), 98.

12. Jonathan Edwards, "The Most High a Prayer-Hearing God," in *The Works of Jonathan Edwards* (Edinburgh: Banner of Truth, 1974), 2:114.

field in which we labor. Naturally our souls are extremely aggravated and shaken up by criticism. Verbal flak makes for very noisy and restless souls, keeping us awake at night and plaguing our thoughts and emotions throughout the day. But Edwards tells us there is a "great quietness" that accompanies the Godward rest and trust of prayer.

Would you not love to have a soul characterized by peaceful calm in the midst of the violent storms of criticism? Then submit yourself to God in believing prayer. Unburden your soul in His presence. Get low before His sovereign glory, and wait on Him in silence. Say with David, "Thou art my hiding place; thou shalt preserve me from trouble; thou shalt compass me about with songs of deliverance" (Ps. 32:7). "As for God, his way is perfect: the word of the LORD is tried: he is a buckler to all those that trust in him" (Ps. 18:30).

In God's wisdom, there is a certain reciprocity involved here. Criticism expands the soul to pray, and prayer expands the soul to endure criticism. Verbal critique should drive us to seek after God. William Cowper's poem captures this well:

> Trials make the promise sweet;
> Trials give new life to prayer;
> Trials bring me to his feet,
> Lay me low, and keep me there.[13]

God uses criticism to breathe new life into our praying. But as we pray, our souls are also refreshed in God, renewed with love, and refocused on Christ. In this way, prayer enables us to bear up under the otherwise crushing weight of criticism.

Pastor, examine yourself at this point. Does criticism impel you to pray? Does it have an enlivening or deadening influence

---

13. William Cowper, "'Tis My Happiness Below," 1774.

on your prayer life? And does your praying reorient your perspective, helping you to respond to criticism with Christlike peace and love?

Prayer's Priority

The priority of our praying should be souls, not situations.[14] Yes, there is a place to pray for your circumstances, but the condition of the hearts involved in those circumstances should have precedence. It is not wrong to pray for vindication when falsely criticized. It is not wrong to pray that God would silence our critics or turn an unfavorable situation to our favor. This is especially the case when God's glory is at stake (see, for example, 2 Kings 19). But circumstances ought not to be the dominant concern of our prayers.

Pray for your own soul. When critical words are directed at you, cry out to God with the psalmist, "Search me, O God, and know my heart: try me, and know my thoughts: And see if there be any wicked way in me, and lead me in the way everlasting" (Ps. 139:23–24). Ask God to not only search you with regards to the content of the criticism, but also with regards to your response to the criticism. Expose your soul to His holy presence and allow Him to graciously convict you of areas where change is needed. Pray as well that He would give you discernment to know how best to respond and that He would purify your motives in doing so.

Pray for your critics. Don't just pray that God would silence them or thwart their purposes. Pray that God would do good for their souls. Seek their eternal welfare before your Father in heaven. We need to recognize that a far greater threat than the criticism we receive is the bitterness that can subtly take root in our hearts toward our critics. D. A. Carson rightly states, "It is

---

14. See Dane C. Ortlund, *Edwards on the Christian Life: Alive to the Beauty of God* (Wheaton, IL: Crossway, 2014), 118–19.

very hard to pray with compassion and zeal for someone we much prefer to resent."[15] How easily our hearts can be blackened with negativity toward our critics. But it is difficult to hold a grudge against a person for whom you sincerely pray. The Lord delivered Job from hard feelings toward his judgmental friends when he interceded on their behalf. John Newton counsels, "As to your opponent, I wish, that, before you set pen to paper against him, and during the whole time you are preparing your answer, you may commend him by earnest prayer to the Lord's teaching and blessing. This practice will have a direct tendency to conciliate your heart to love and pity him."[16]

Consistent prayer for the good of our critics will fill our hearts with love and compassion toward them, make us more receptive to their critiques, and enable us to respond in a way that magnifies Jesus Christ.

BE PATIENT

When we lack biblical sobriety, we will lack patience in the face of criticism. We will be quick to lash out, quick to defend, and quick to clean up the mess made of our reputation. This is the very opposite of a sober response. The sobriety that accompanies a mind renewed by God's truth will generally take its time in responding.

The Twenty-Four Hour Rule

It is not uncommon for critique to come at the worst times. For pastors, this is typically Monday morning. You have completely spent yourself intellectually, emotionally, and physically

15. D. A. Carson, *Praying with Paul: A Call to Spiritual Reformation,* 2nd ed. (Grand Rapids: Baker Academic, 2014), 99.
16. John Newton, "Letter XIX: On Controversy," *The Works of John Newton* (London, 1808), 1:241.

on the Lord's Day, often preaching two sermons, teaching Sunday school or catechism class, counseling, and showing hospitality. And on Monday morning you receive a critical email or phone call. When this happens, delay your response if at all possible. Tell the person you appreciate their concern and ask them if you can have a day or two to think it over. It is not wise to respond to criticism when you are psychologically expended. It may be best to read no negative emails or text messages until Tuesday morning!

Even if you receive criticism at a time when you are strong emotionally and physically, it is still a good general rule not to respond to weighty criticism for at least twenty-four hours. This provides you with time to reflect and pray, get past some of the hurt, and consult others whose wisdom you respect. Rarely is there a need to respond to criticism immediately. If it is possible to delay, then delay! Not only will this give you an opportunity to cool down and contemplate, but it will give your critic the opportunity to do the same.

Neither Hasty, Nor Heedless

Remember, you are known more for your *reactions* than your *actions* (see Prov. 16:32). Forcing solutions to issues too hastily may make a bad situation worse. Some situations will yield only to the healing touch of time. Truth has a way of vindicating itself over time. If you walk with integrity before God and your church members, most—not all, but most—criticisms will fade after a month or two. Luke 21:19 says, "In your patience possess ye your souls."

The call to patience, however, is not a call to neglect responding. There are times to not give a verbal response to criticism at all, but when such a response is needed, it should not be delayed beyond the time necessary to pray and process. If you are heedless and fail to seek resolution, it will only serve to increase the tension and probably multiply the amount of verbal criticism you receive. Suddenly you will not only be a poor preacher, but a poor preacher who doesn't care to deal with the fact. If you have told your critic you would contact them the following day, make sure to keep your word and do it. Do not unnecessarily prolong responding. It will prove to be your undoing.

BE PRUDENT

How do we know when a verbal response is necessary? Great prudence is needed to determine when to remain silent and when to reply.

When Criticism Calls for Silence

Sometimes the best response to criticism is silence. Our wordlessness can speak volumes, often more than our words. Silence is not a failure to respond, but a particular way of responding to criticism. In certain situations, it is the most appropriate way to respond. This is especially the case when facing destructive criticism. Spurgeon writes, "To all honest and just remarks we are bound to give due measure of heed, but to the bitter verdict of prejudice, the frivolous faultfinding of men of fashion, the stupid utterances of the ignorant, and the fierce denunciations of opponents, we may very safely turn a deaf ear."[17]

Some accusations leveled against us are clearly preposterous and ill-willed. Those critiques will be immediately recognized as groundless by people who know us. Even people who know us very little will sense in the critic's speech a hatred and arrogance that contradicts the gospel. In such situations, we need to exercise a certain deafness, humbly ignoring the criticism. This deaf ear should be accompanied by mute lips.

---

17. Charles H. Spurgeon, *Lectures to My Students* (repr., Peabody, MA: Hendrickson Publishers, 2010), 351.

A respectful silence can be tremendously effective. Often ill-willed critics want nothing more than to get us riled up and in defensive mode. Giving a verbal response would only fan the flame of their negative intentions toward us. Don't get side-tracked into fruitless controversy, or spend your energy trying to appease or persuade implacable critics who thrive on animosity. Refuse to sink to the level of such a critic; don't render evil for evil. Fight God's battles, not your own, and you will discover that He will fight yours. It is not for you to repay. "Dearly beloved, avenge not yourselves, but rather give place unto wrath: for it is written, Vengeance is mine; I will repay, saith the Lord" (Rom. 12:19).

Ill-informed and ill-willed verbal flak has a way of self-destructing over time. If you continue walking with God in integrity, most criticism will die out eventually. Again Spurgeon, in his characteristic color, states, "A great lie, if unnoticed is like a big fish out of water, it dashes and plunges and beats itself to death in a short time. To answer it is to supply it with its element, and help it to a longer life. Falsehoods usually carry their own refutation somewhere about them, and sting themselves to death."[18] The best thing to do in such cases is to leave the critic and the criticism alone. Seeking justification or self-defense will only prolong the life of the criticism.

Once when I was in a restaurant with my wife asking her counsel on whether or not I should answer a certain criticism, I picked up a pack of sugar. On the back it said, "Never explain; your friends don't need it, and your enemies won't believe you anyhow."[19] Though this is not always true, of course, a general rule in ministry is that those who are genuinely for your ministry won't need your self-justification; they will see right through the

18. Spurgeon, 353.
19. This quote is attributed to Elbert Hubbard.

criticism. And your enemies won't buy into your self-justification; your defensiveness will only stimulate further attack. Silence can be our great weapon in such instances.

Silence can also be the best solution for situations that you have tried to resolve repeatedly in vain. When a friend and his family left our church in opposition to me and my shortcomings some years ago, I tried hard and long to win them back—but all seemed futile. Finally, I called a ministerial friend in Illinois for advice. He listened well to the entire story—to my own faults and weaknesses as well as my former friend's responses to my overtures. Then he said something I never have forgotten: "Joel, you have tried your hardest to win them back. You have begged God to bless your efforts. Now it is time for you to surrender this all to God, remembering that Proverbs 18:19 says that 'a brother offended is harder to be won than a strong city.' You need to remember now that you have seven hundred fifty other souls to care for. Surrender this to the Lord, and move on with ministering to your sheep who have not left you." I followed that advice and found peace. And though this friend never returned to the church I serve, he eventually made peace with me, by God's grace, at His time and in His way.

When Criticism Calls for Speech

Is it ever necessary to respond verbally to unjust or destructive criticism? Yes, there are times when to fail to lift up our voices would be dishonoring to God. In expounding and applying the ninth commandment, the Westminster divines include the following duties:

- Preserving and promoting truth between man and man, and the good name of our neighbor, as well as our own,
- Appearing and standing for the truth,
- Discouraging talebearers, flatterers, and slanderers,

- Loving and caring for our own good name, and defending it when need requires.[20]

It is not without significance that twice our forefathers emphasized the need to preserve and defend "our own good name." The ninth commandment, in its negative denouncement of falsehood, positively calls us to the promotion of truth. This makes it our responsibility and duty to ensure our names are not unjustly dragged through the mud. Such is especially the case for the gospel minister, seeing that he is an ambassador of Jesus Christ. So how do we know when to respond to destructive or untruthful criticism? If the ninth commandment charges us to promote the truth, then we need to carefully consider what response will serve that end.

As stated above, in cases where the criticism is obviously slanderous, silence is often the best way to promote the truth. After a painful church discipline case wherein a woman was excommunicated for unrepentantly cheating on and divorcing her husband, this woman proceeded to slander the pastor. She quietly spread rumors that he was having an affair with another woman in the congregation. The pastor brought the accusation to the elders and they decided it was best not to publicly respond. Why? Because this woman had a track record of deceit and her accusation was groundless. Those to whom she was spreading this lie saw it clearly for what it was. Slander of this sort is self-destructive. Thus, the best way to promote the truth is to leave the lie to kill itself.

In cases where false accusations may exercise great influence, it is our duty to speak up for the good of our name and the glory of God. Ask yourself these questions:

---

20. See Westminster Larger Catechism, question and answer 144.

- Will people be swayed by these lies? Will some be led to forfeit the truth if I don't speak up?
- Is my critic well respected? Will people be prone to listen to them merely because of their name or position?
- Does this accusation have the potential to cause my people to question my integrity? Left unchecked could it seriously undermine my ministry?
- Who is the audience of this slander? Is it my congregation? My enemies? People with whom I have little or no acquaintance? Is it far-reaching in scope?

These will not always be easy questions to answer. But where there is potential for truth to be forfeited, your reputation assassinated, your ministry subverted, and your people deluded, then it is your duty (or the duty of your elders) to lift up a voice in response.

The apostle Paul understood this duty. He had planted various churches in the southern region of Galatia on his first missionary journey (see Acts 13–14). But shortly after his departure, false teachers had infiltrated the churches, proclaiming another gospel. By their critical words, the Judaizers sought to undermine Paul's apostolic authority as a means of undermining his message. They placed a large question mark over his character and calling. For Paul this was no small thing, not because he had an unhealthy preoccupation with his reputation, but because he understood that if the messenger is slandered, then the message is subverted. Thus, roughly one third of his Epistle to the Galatians consists of a defense of himself and his ministry, dealing with the slanderous lies of these ill-intentioned wolves (see Gal. 1–2).

It requires prudence to know when to speak and when to remain silent in the face of destructive criticism, but criticism that is constructive, legitimate, and good-intentioned, especially if coming from one of our own sheep, always requires a verbal response. If, after examining yourself before the Lord, you find the criticism to be true, even in part, be quick to confess your sin, mistake, or weakness to your critic. If the situation warrants, ask for their forgiveness and prayers. But if after prayerfully pondering the criticism and seeking counsel from others, you are convinced that your good-intentioned critic is flat-out wrong, graciously and humbly seek to explain your perspective to the critic—with an open Bible. Seek mutual understanding, even if mutual agreement is not possible.

When a verbal response is needed, it is always best to give one face-to-face. You may think email is a better way to respond because it will enable you to slowly craft and edit clear statements without the nervousness and unpredictability that might accompany a face-to-face meeting. But even the clearest email can easily lead to misunderstanding because your critic is unable to hear the tone of your voice, see the warmth of your facial expressions, and ask clarifying questions. Communicating by phone is better than email, but it too should be avoided when it is feasible to meet your critic in person. Where the circumstances will not permit such a meeting, a video call is probably the best alternative. The point is that you want your response to be as personal as possible.

GIRD UP YOUR MIND

If the Word of Christ is dwelling richly in us, then our chief concern in responding to criticism will be to do so at the time and in the way that will best exalt the glory of God and promote His enjoyment among all peoples. The sober mind that is girded up with prayerfulness, patience, and prudence brings great glory to God and good to His church in the face of criticism.

6

RESPOND WITH GRACE

As pastors we need supernatural strength to withstand the verbal attacks that come our way. While our work requires lamblike meekness, it equally requires lionlike resilience. Without it, we will not last long-term in the pastoral ministry. This kind of strength is not conjured up naturally but is found through the means of grace—that is, in supernatural communion with the One in whom there is "grace upon grace" (John 1:16 ESV). It is the super-abounding grace of Christ alone that enables us to respond to criticism with the right kind of strength. Such gracious strength will be realized in our lives and ministries only as we maintain a clean conscience in Him, learn from the school of criticism in Him, and love our critics in Him.

KEEP A CLEAN CONSCIENCE UNDER GRACE

A clean conscience is vital for ministers of the gospel. Our consciences are gifts from God. They are internal alarms that alert us when we are not living according to God's righteous will. Of course, the conscience is not infallible, and it has the potential to lead us astray. Because of sin, conscience stands in need of gospel recalibration to deliver from overactive legalism (i.e., conviction for that which is not actually sinful—which some Puritans called "an overly scrupulous conscience") or an underactive antinomianism (i.e., no conviction for that which is actually sinful). But when our consciences are ordered by God's truth and washed in Christ's blood, they are an immense help to us.[1]

Drawing from the biblical evidence, Pastor Albert Martin demonstrates that a clear conscience before God is the fruit of three characteristics.[2] First, there is no known disobedience that has not been confessed and repented of. We must be quick in dealing with our sin, taking our souls to Christ for forgiving, cleansing, and empowering grace. Second, there is no God-given duty that we are consciously neglecting or failing to carry out by His grace. We willingly and joyfully live as servants of God, seeking to be faithful stewards of that which He has entrusted to us. Third, there is no revealed truth that we reject, suppress, or water down for selfish ends. A clear conscience requires not only orthopraxy (sound living), but also orthodoxy (sound doctrine). In short, such a conscience can be possessed only as we abide in Christ, living in devotion to Him and His Word.

The role of the conscience in coping with criticism could have easily fit into previous chapters. Why include it here? Because if we would respond to criticism with grace and strength, we must possess a conscience void of offense.

The Boldness of a Clean Conscience

The apostle Paul was no stranger to slander. As he stood on trial before Felix, the governor of Caesarea, his enemies falsely

---

1. For further study on conscience, see Joel R. Beeke and Mark Jones, "The Puritans on Conscience," in *A Puritan Theology: Doctrine for Life* (Grand Rapids: Reformation Heritage Books, 2012), 909–26; Andrew David Naselli and J. D. Crowley, *Conscience: What It Is, How to Train It, and Loving Those Who Differ* (Wheaton, IL: Crossway, 2016).

2. Albert N. Martin, *Pastoral Theology*, vol. 1, *The Man of God: His*

accused him, painting the blackest picture imaginable (see Acts 24:1–9). Paul's response is remarkable. It is characterized by gracious strength, meekly exposing the lies of his opponents and using the opportunity to proclaim Christ, knowing that the gospel was the real reason he had been put on trial (see Acts 24:10–21).

What kept him from cowering in the face of his critics? What enabled him to respond with integrity and truth? He tells us in the middle of his defense: "And herein do I exercise myself, to have always a conscience void of offence toward God, and toward men" (v. 16). There was no known controversy in his life toward God or man left undealt with. He labored diligently to maintain a clear conscience. Men were accusing him, but his conscience was acquitting him. And this produced a soul of lionlike confidence. Puritan Nathaniel Vincent writes, "A good conscience steels a man's heart with courage, and makes him fearless before his enemies."[3]

Is this not what upheld Martin Luther at the Diet of Worms? On April 17, 1521, the German Reformer stood before the emperor, "the most powerful man in the world, who was surrounded by a large group of powerful people from both the church and the empire."[4] Luther was called on to recant a table of his published works. The stakes were high, and Luther understood that his failure to retract his writings would likely lead to his death. But on the following day, he humbly declared that he could not recant unless convinced from Scripture. Why? Because it would violate his conscience: "My conscience is captive to the Word of God. I cannot and will not recant anything, for to go against

Calling and Godly Life (Montville, NJ: Trinity Pulpit Press, 2018), 274.

3. Nathaniel Vincent, *Heaven upon Earth* (London: for Thomas Parkhurst, 1676), 306.

4. Herman Selderhuis, *Martin Luther: A Spiritual Biography* (Wheaton, IL: Crossway, 2017), 156.

conscience is neither right nor safe."[5] While Luther admitted that his writings had been overly harsh at points and were certainly not infallible, he was convinced they contained the truth of God and could not renounce them. He had a clear conscience before God and would rather die than violate it. This enabled him to stand courageously against the most powerful men in the world.

If we are consciously walking in integrity before God, in dependence on His Spirit and in submission to His Word, there will be a sense of God's smile on us. In his diary entry "On Suffering Injuries," the renowned English evangelical minister Charles Simeon wrote of one such experience of coping with criticism:

> I have this moment heard of a most malignant attempt to injure my character: and I take up my pen to record, to the praise and glory of God, that my soul is kept in perfect peace. I pity those who delight in the exercise of such wicked dispositions. Little do they think that they injure themselves more than me, and that there is a day coming when the righteousness of the righteous shall be upon him, and the wickedness of the wicked shall be upon him. It is an unspeakable consolation that God knoweth every thing, and will judge [with] righteous judgment. To Him I can make my appeal, that in the point referred to I am greatly injured: but whilst I have the testimony of my own conscience and light of my Redeemer's countenance, none of these things do move me, or ought to move me.[6]

How seemingly insignificant the frowns of men appear when we are aware of the beaming countenance of our heavenly Father on us! "For the eyes of the LORD run to and fro throughout the

5. Roland H. Bainton, *Here I Stand: A Life of Martin Luther* (New York: Abingdon-Cokesbury Press, 1950), 185.

6. *Memoirs of the Rev. Charles Simeon, with a Selection from His Writings,* abridged by J. S. Stone and William Carus (New York: Protestant Episcopal

whole earth, to shew himself strong in the behalf of them whose heart is perfect toward him" (2 Chron. 16:9). Oh to have the favorable eyes of God on us, for in His favor is life itself (see Ps. 30:5)! What could more steel our hearts in the face of criticism? What could better enable us to respond in God-fearing strength?

The Love of a Clean Conscience

The boldness of a clean conscience does not bulldoze opponents; it is a gracious strength marked by love. Paul, in his First Epistle to Timothy, exhorted him to "charge some that they teach no other doctrine" (1 Tim. 1:3). There were false teachers posing a threat to this infant church, and Timothy needed to exercise his authority to prevent them from undermining the gospel. The apostle clarified his concerns: "The aim of our charge is love that issues from a pure heart and a good conscience and a sincere faith" (1:5 ESV). Timothy was to deal with these agitators to the end that they might repent, leading to a genuine love for God and His people. And such love, he explained, "issues from a pure heart and a good conscience and a sincere faith." A healthy conscience is productive of love.[7] William Hendriksen, commenting on this passage, writes, "A *conscience* cleared of guilt and made obedient to God's law will begin to approve only such thoughts, words, and deeds . . . which are in harmony with the one, summarizing aim of that law, namely, *love*."[8]

The joy of a conscience void of offense is unspeakably sweet. This is a joy that the greatest trials and the harshest criticism cannot undo. It is a joy found in God and the felt sense of His favorable disposition toward us in Christ. It is the joy of assurance of

---

Society for the Promotion of Evangelical Knowledge, 1859), 239.

7. Of course, there is a certain circularity here since a good conscience is the product of a life of love to God and people (i.e., obedience to the law).

8. William Hendriksen, *Exposition of the Pastoral Epistles*, Baker New Testament Commentary (Grand Rapids: Baker, 1957), 61.

His love, flowing from a life of holiness. And being experientially acquainted with God's love for us, we will be enabled to love others, even our fiercest critics. Thomas Murphy writes, "When earnest godliness reigns within it turns the whole life of the minister into a work of love. . . . There may be apparent drawbacks to his comfort arising from poverty, or opposition of unreasonable men, or want of honor from the world, but all is more than made up by his hidden springs of spiritual joy. . . . The approbation of conscience will be to him a perpetual feast."[9]

A clear conscience, resulting from a holy life in Christ, is "a perpetual feast" for the minister. As he walks conscious of God's favorable disposition toward him, he will be disposed to show grace and favor to others. Drawing from "his hidden springs of spiritual joy," he will be animated with Spirit-wrought, Christlike love for his critics. He will have no need for carnal self-defense when he has God's smile on him. Such a conscience liberates you to love your critics.

The Uncompromising Character of a Clean Conscience

Do you know the "perpetual feast" of a conscience void of offense before God and man? Are there sins in your life that you are failing to deal with? Are there duties you are willfully neglecting? Are there divine truths you are quelling to appease yourself or your people?

If you would know the deep joy of a clean conscience, you must commit yourself by God's grace to an uncompromising pursuit of holiness. This is especially so behind closed doors. What you are in the privacy of your home and heart reveals your true self.

---

9. Thomas Murphy, *Pastoral Theology: The Pastor in the Various Duties of His Office* (repr., Willow Street, PA: Old Paths Publications, 1996), 55–56.

- *In your home*
  - Are you selflessly loving your wife and children?
  - Are you quick to ask their forgiveness when you wrong them and zealous in performing the duties God has called you to as a husband and father?
- *In your study*
  - Are you using your time in a way that honors the Lord and serves the church?
  - Are you looking at sexually promiscuous material on your computer?
  - Do you do anything behind the closed door of your office that you would be ashamed of your people knowing about?
- *In your heart*
  - Are you quick to take your sin to the fount open for sin and uncleanness?
  - Is there any sin you are not willing to unconditionally forsake?
  - Is there any area where you have justified compromise?
  - Are you actively pursuing purity of mind and intention?
  - Is there unaddressed spiritual apathy, lethargy, and complacency in your soul?
  - Do you preach to yourself what you preach to your people?
  - Shortcomings notwithstanding, is your life a transcript of your sermons?

Pastor, be assured that your integrity in private will directly affect your response to criticism. If you are a man of moral compromise and one who places little value on the smile of God, you will know little of gracious strength in the face of verbal critique.

Commit yourself to God afresh. Repent of any and every area of known compromise. Resolve by God's grace to live in holiness before God and man. Charles Hodge exhorted his students at Princeton:

> Do endeavor to be honest men, men of unquestionable integrity, on whose word everyone can implicitly rely, of whose purity of motive and purpose no one can doubt. Impress deeply upon your mind that morality is a great part of religion, a great and essential part of the service which we owe to God. Habituate yourselves always to look at the moral character of everything you are called upon to do. Determine always to do what is right, regardless of consequences. Never trifle with your moral feelings; it is trifling with God. Never suffer yourselves to do wrong in little matters; to neglect little duties; but be punctual and faithful in all engagements, and obligations.[10]

Our mantra ought to be "No compromise!" Then we will be able to say with Paul in the face of criticism, "For our rejoicing is this, the testimony of our conscience, that in simplicity and godly sincerity, not with fleshly wisdom, but by the grace of God, we have had our conversation in the world, and more abundantly to you-ward" (2 Cor. 1:12).

ENROLL IN THE GRACIOUS SCHOOL OF CRITICISM

If we are living under the smile of God, we will learn to see criticism as a grace from His fatherly hand. Verbal critique is a tool that God uses to fashion His children after the image of His Son. Seeing that ministers of the gospel are called to an

---

10. Charles Hodge, "The Character Traits of the Gospel Minister," in *Princeton and the Work of the Christian Ministry*, ed. James M. Garretson (Edinburgh: Banner of Truth Trust, 2012), 2:138.

exemplary life of holiness, we ought to expect God to subject us to criticism more than the ordinary believer. God enrolls His under-shepherds in the school of criticism in order to teach them many invaluable lessons.

I Think Far Too Highly of Myself

Archibald Alexander once wrote, "Too much applause is a dangerous thing to a young minister."[11] While this is particularly the case for the new pastor, it remains the case for the seasoned veteran in the ministry. Few things could be more to our detriment than the perpetual praise of our fellowman. We are so easily puffed up and led into self-congratulations for *our* ministerial successes. We are so quick to look in the mirror and to be impressed by what we see. This is why David Powlison confesses, "If I only listen to my allies, or to yes-men, clones, devotees, and fellow factionaries, then I might as well inject narcotics into my veins."[12] Similarly, Spurgeon writes, "Have you not by this time discovered that flattery is as injurious as it is pleasant? It softens the mind and makes you more sensitive to slander. In proportion as praise pleases you censure will pain you. Besides, it is a crime to be taken off from your great object of glorifying the Lord Jesus by petty considerations as to your little self, and, if there were no other reason, this ought to weigh much with you. Pride is a deadly sin, and will grow without your borrowing the parish water cart to quicken it."[13] How true this is! We stand in grave need of criticism if we would be delivered from ourselves.

---

11. Quoted in Iain H. Murray, *Revival & Revivalism: The Making and Marring of American Evangelicalism 1750–1858* (Edinburgh: Banner of Truth Trust, 1994), 8.

12. David Powlison, "Does the Shoe Fit?" *Journal of Biblical Counseling* (Spring 2002): 3.

13. Charles Spurgeon, *Lectures to My Students* (repr., Peabody, MA:

The Lord uses verbal critique to bring us down from our self-constructed pedestals. He wields constructive criticism to expose our blind spots. By it we are reminded that we have not arrived as saints or as ministers of the gospel. We have made but a small beginning in our growth in grace and the cultivation of our God-given gifts. We are not as great a preacher as we imagined ourselves to be. We have not been as faithful in the discharge of our duties as perhaps we imagined. We are not as holy as we suspected. By criticism, high thoughts of self are brought low. This is equally true of destructive criticism. Even when it is untrue, verbal critique exposes our hearts and reveals what is really inside, as a means by which God humbles us in the dust. The reality is that all of us think far too highly of ourselves. And one lesson God graciously seeks to teach us is that we are not as great as we think.

I Care Far Too Much about Myself

Coupled with our high estimation of self is that we care far too deeply about our reputations. As we saw in chapter 4, pride is not content to be the best but wants everyone to reckon with the fact that it is the best. We care deeply about how others perceive us. We want to be esteemed and praised. Concern for our own reputation often consumes us. William Perkins reveals the idolatry of our hearts in this:

> It gives us a taste and view of our own natural pride and self-love. For when we hear God dishonored by swearing or our neighbor's name defamed by slandering, we are not only not grieved but oftentimes are the cause thereof and take great delight therein, especially in hearing other men's faults ripped up to their disgrace, but yet we can in no sort brook or suffer our own good name to be called in question. If ourselves be

Hendrickson Publishers, 2010), 352.

evil spoken of, we are presently filled with malice and envy, and cannot be at rest till we be requited or revenged.[14]

God uses criticism to reveal the idol of self. We are deeply concerned, hurt, and angered when our reputation is marred. But what about the Lord's reputation? Does blasphemy disturb us to the core of our being? When people falsely accuse God or shake their fists in hatred at him, are we grieved? We shed many tears over the defacing of our own reputation, but what about God's? Can we say with the psalmist, "Rivers of waters run down mine eyes, because they keep not thy law" (Ps. 119:136)? When it comes to our spiritual brothers or sisters or fellow ministers of the gospel, are our souls agitated when their names are undermined? God uses criticism to show us that we care far too deeply about ourselves and to cause us to relinquish control of our reputation and to grow in our concern for God and others.

I Am an Under-Shepherd, Not the Chief Shepherd

If you remain at a church for any period of time, it is almost inevitable that some from your congregation will grow so critical of your ministry that they will leave the church. Often the people you invest ample amount of time, energy, and love into will be the ones who later desert you. Why would God permit this to happen? Peter Lillback, reflecting on his own experience in the ministry, writes, "I had to learn that the members of the church are not mine, but Christ's."[15] When the people of God criticize us and leave us, we are freshly reminded that they are not ours. We are under-shepherds, not the Chief Shepherd. The deep pain of

14. William Perkins, "Sermon on the Mount," in *The Works of William Perkins*, ed. J. Stephen Yuille (Grand Rapids: Reformation Heritage Books, 2014), 1:594–95.

15. Peter A. Lillback, *Saint Peter's Principles: Leadership for Those Who Already Know Their Incompetence* (Phillipsburg, NJ: P&R, 2019), 355.

losing sheep and the sharp words of criticism teach us that our people ultimately belong to Jesus.

I Desperately Need the Lord

The fires of criticism also remind us just how needy we really are. We are prone to grow quite self-sufficient. We can carry out our ministerial duties with little sense of our profound poverty of spirit. But when criticism comes, it exposes our weaknesses and sins. And by so doing, it impresses on us our acute need of the gospel. Criticism is a God-given impetus to intensify our grip on Christ. Oh how desperately we stand in need of His righteousness and His empowering grace!

This is particularly true in the weekly marathon of preparing new sermons. At times, persevering in prayerful sermon preparation when wounded by severe criticism seems nearly impossible. At other times, our great Shepherd lifts the burden from our shoulders and provides humbling insights and illumination that comfort us—in ways that Christ increases while we decrease—during the very act of sermon preparation. When that is the case, we usually preach the following Lord's Day with more freedom and unction than we preach those sermons in which we had little or no experiential engagements or holy wrestling.

Are you learning these lessons in the school of criticism? Those who embrace criticism as a grace are enabled to respond in grace. Verbal critique, even if it be slanderous, is a part of the all things that God is working together for your good, that good being your conformity to Christ (see Rom. 8:28–29). Since that is the case, you ought not to be crushed by it. It ought not to debilitate you. There ought to be a quiet strength beneath this gracious rod.

Let criticism drive you out of yourself and to the Lord. He has good purposes in it beyond what you can presently see. He is making you more fit and useful through it. As D. James Kennedy once said, "Let your critics be the watchers after your soul, the beneficiaries of your career. Let them help you along the way."[16] Learn to see criticism as an assistant in your sanctification and in ministerial fruitfulness. Learn to see critics as gracious blessings from God, used to keep you from high-mindedness and compromise. Train your soul to reflexively receive criticism as a grace in the very moments it is being dished out.

EMBRACE THE CRITIC WITH GRACE

Critics are gifts from the hand of God. This is true of faithful church members who critique us for our betterment, as well as enemies who seek to vilify us. Though we do not embrace all criticism as true, we need to embrace all critics with grace. Often our critics don't deserve our kindness, but that is the point. Grace is unmerited, even demerited, favor.

The Greatest of These Is Love

Our natural tendency is to treat our critics with a vengeance. But when we see them under God's gracious government, we are enabled to respond to them in love. Many truths already discussed, including listening to your critic, praying for them, and receiving their critique, could easily fit under this section. These are all ways in which we embrace our critics in love. Here, however, we want to focus not so much on the outward acts of love, but the inward disposition of love toward our critics.

Loving our *constructive* critics ought not to be overly difficult, though our pride can often prevent us from doing so. Proverbs 27:6 tells us, "Faithful are the wounds of a friend." When a critic

16. D. James Kennedy, "How to Handle Criticism," *Christian Observer* (Feb. 22, 1991): 3.

wounds us for our good, it is a tremendous blessing. We need to remember how difficult it is to give constructive criticism. When we truly love someone, we don't desire to inflict pain on them. But our caring critics are willing to do the difficult work of wounding us. They love us enough to critique us. They love us enough to not allow us to remain as we are. This ought to cause our souls to love them all the more. How strange it would be to hate those who love us enough to willingly step out of their comfort zone to criticize us!

If you find it hard to love your loving critics, how much more your hostile critics. "Love for enemies," writes Ed Welch, "is the pinnacle of Christian obedience to God."[17] When enemies seek our demise by their hateful words, it is here that the maturity of our faith is tested. It is in these fires that the genuineness of our Christianity is proved. Remember what Christ commands you to do: "Rejoice, and be exceeding glad" (Matt. 5:12).

True faith "worketh by love" (Gal. 5:6). Such love is no respecter of persons, reaching even to our most vicious opponents (see Matt. 5:44). How does faith produce such love? It eyes Christ. It sees the God-man who willingly laid down His life for His enemies. It embraces the One who by His self-giving love has made His enemies to be His friends. And it reckons with such truth not as a vague generality, but as an intensely personal reality. By faith, we come to see that we were indeed enemies of God and as such He lavished undeserved affection on us, reconciling us to Himself. Being the recipients of such love, how could we not extend love to our hateful critics? Faith receives the love of Christ and for that reason cannot help but produce love.

17. Edward T. Welch, *When People Are Big and God Is Small: Overcoming Peer Pressure, Codependency, and the Fear of Man* (Phillipsburg, NJ: P&R, 1997), 190.

Our critics have not injured us even one percent as much as we have injured Christ with our sins, and yet He loves us with an unchangeable love. Is this not the grand secret and the greatest of all helps in coping with criticism? Isn't this precisely the point of the parable of the unforgiving servant told in Matthew 18:23–35? If Christ has forgiven us millions of sins against Him (for all sin is against Him), can we not forgive our critic for one or even a few handfuls of sin against us?

Try this out: the next time you are starting to grieve over criticism and feel anger rise within you against your critic, stop and meditate on how you have treated Christ all your life. We can almost guarantee that your ability to cope with criticism at that moment will rise substantively.

We ought to feel compassion for our destructive critics. We ought to fear for their souls rather than for our reputations. Their hateful, critical spirit places them in grave spiritual danger. It also makes them exceedingly unhappy. The life of a chronic critic is a miserable one. The cup is always half empty. Everything is seen through the grey lens of negativity. And what damage habitually critical adults do to their children. How seldom do such children become stalwart sons and daughters of the church! Be grateful to God that you are on the receiving end, not the criticizing end— negative critics are in a woeful condition. Pity such a one.

Matthew Henry provides us with a wise example of how to use compassion. When a thief robbed his wallet, he thanked the Lord that it was only his wallet that was taken and not his life, and that he was the one robbed rather than the robber. Compassion helps us to take the focus off "poor me" and to put the focus on the genuinely poor, negative, and destructive critic.

On an annual family visitation, the father of the home began to blatantly criticize me to my face in front of his wife and several children. When I suggested that perhaps we could finish the visit first with the children and then talk together, he replied matter-of-factly, "That won't be necessary, pastor, because all of the criticisms I have against you, my children have heard numerous times." I could feel anger rise within me; I felt like striking back by telling him what a foolish father he was for poisoning the minds of his children with his negativity. As I drove home that night, I was feeling sorry for myself in a mega way, when suddenly the thought dawned, *I should be feeling sorry for him and not myself, as his attitude has the potential to ruin his family.* Then, compassion drove me to begin to pray earnestly for him, his wife, and his children.

As You Have Been Forgiven

We must put away anything that inhibits love toward our critics. As Peter directs us, lay aside "all malice, and all guile, and hypocrisies, and envies, and all evil speakings" (1 Peter 2:1). You must watch carefully over your heart, not allowing a bitter spirit to develop. Bitterness is a subtle sin. Our hearts can grow cold and indifferent to our critics. We can even begin to despise them and desire their demise. But a heart of love will not hold a grudge, nor will it harbor malicious thoughts. Examine yourself here. Would it bring you joy if your critic was publicly shamed or exposed? Do you desire the spiritual good of your critic?

The call to love does not mean you need to—or even should—have warm, fuzzy feelings inside when you think of your critic. But if you have been verbally wronged, your calling is to imitate Christ: "And be ye kind one to another, tenderhearted, forgiving one another, even as God for Christ's sake hath forgiven you" (Eph. 4:32). We must offer grace and forgiveness unconditionally just as Christ has to us. That being said, we cannot actually grant forgiveness until the person has repented (see Luke 17:3–4). Christ offers forgiveness to all unconditionally, but He actually forgives a person on the conditions of faith and repentance. As Chris Brauns wisely notes, "Christian forgiveness is a commitment to the repentant."[18] But whether our unjust critics actually repent or seek to put things right, we need to have a forgiving disposition toward them, giving the offense to God and not harboring bitter thoughts toward them. We need to be ready to receive them with open arms, forgiving them in our own hearts even if the condition of repentance has not yet been attained from our critic's side. We must take care not to become critics of our critics!

GRACE UPON GRACE

As we strive by grace to keep our consciences clean and learn the lessons of criticism, we will be enabled to stand strong and embrace our critics with grace. As our Savior is full of "grace upon grace," so too will we be. Let our responses to criticism not contradict the gospel of grace that we proclaim.

18. Chris Brauns, *Unpacking Forgiveness: Biblical Answers for Complex Questions and Deep Wounds* (Wheaton, IL: Crossway, 2008), 57. Space does not permit us to expand on this topic here, but Brauns's book is an excellent place to start if you wish to read further on the subject. He defines forgiveness as "a commitment by the offended to pardon graciously the repentant from moral liability and to be reconciled to that person, though not all consequences are necessarily eliminated" (p. 55).

PART 3

PRACTICAL PRINCIPLES FOR CONSTRUCTIVE CRITICISM IN THE CHURCH

7

GIVING CONSTRUCTIVE CRITIQUE TO OTHERS

We have spent the last six chapters focused on coping with criticism in the ministry. As pastors, we need great wisdom to navigate the turbulent waters of just and unjust criticism directed our way. But it is equally imperative that we learn how to constructively critique others.

Ministers are to be the sanctified agents of criticism, not merely the targets. The gospel records of Christ's earthly ministry, as well as the epistles, are everywhere strewn with conflict. Much of the work of Jesus and His apostles consisted in confrontation and rebuke for the glory of God. Paul explains that the God-breathed Word "is profitable for doctrine, for reproof, for correction, for instruction in righteousness" (2 Tim. 3:16). We happily wield the Scriptures for doctrine and instruction in righteousness, but there is something in us that cringes when it comes to correction and reproof. Yet this is precisely what we are to do: "Preach the word; be instant in season, out of season; reprove, rebuke, exhort with all long suffering and doctrine" (2 Tim. 4:2). So long as our people continue in this age with remaining sin in their hearts, they stand in need of this chastening use of the Word through our public preaching and private counseling.

Perhaps there has never been a time in history when the temptation has been greater to compromise at this point. Relativism is the ruling dogma of our culture. We are tolerated so long as we don't tell others they are wrong. How arrogant do you have to be to actually believe that you have a monopoly on truth and morality? Though we reject the rejection of universals, we may be more influenced by our culture than we realize. The temptation may not be to cast off a Christian worldview or to espouse a form of relativistic postmodernism. It may be much subtler: "I can hold to these beliefs and hold them firmly, so long as I don't force them on others. After all, who am I to tell someone they are wrong?" The Scriptures, however, are plain that a faithful ministry will be one that fearlessly exposes error in doctrine and deed—rebuking, warning, and calling back to the paths of God. To shrink from this task is nothing less than abandoning our God-given duty.

But how are we to do it? We have all seen heavy-handed pastors who appeared to thrive on crushing their sheep with rebukes and reproofs. What does it look like to criticize our people in a Christlike and constructive manner?

While not a Christian, Aristotle had common grace insights that may prove helpful to us at this point. This ancient teacher of rhetoric taught that compelling communication (what he called "persuasion") consists of three elements: ethos, pathos, and logos. He writes, "Of the modes of persuasion furnished by the spoken word there are three kinds. The first kind depends on the personal character [ethos] of the speaker; the second kind on putting the audience into a certain frame of mind [pathos]; the third on proof, or apparent proof, provided by the words of the speech itself [logos]."[1] Constructive criticism is more than

---

1. Aristotle, "Rhetorica," in *The Basic Works of Aristotle,* ed. Richard McKeon (New York: Random House, 1968), 1329.

persuasion, but it is not less than persuasion. We are seeking to convince our target audience of their error and to encourage, yes, even compel them to change. This, of course, is done in dependence on the Spirit, who alone can change hearts and lives. But if we are to constructively critique our people in a way that reflects Jesus Christ, we must possess this triad of ethos, pathos, and logos.

THE ETHOS OF CRITICISM

When criticizing others, our minds are prone to focus almost exclusively on logos—the point we are making, the evidence undergirding our critique, and the rightness of our position.

We can spend hours composing the right words and making sure our logic is tight. Logos is certainly important. But even when the words we speak are perfectly sound and coherent, they will not build up if the other two elements of persuasion are missing.

We must begin where Aristotle does, with ethos. This aspect of persuasion focuses not on the message, but on the messenger. If we would criticize to the glory of God, we must possess a certain credibility. "We are so constituted," writes James Stalker, "that what we hear depends very much for its effect on how we are disposed towards him who speaks."[2] We must be men of integrity and men who have gained the confidence of our people. As pastors, we must be what we are called to be and appear to be to others.

A Holy Ministry

Paul exhorted Christian slaves to live in such a way as to "adorn the doctrine of God our Saviour" (Titus 2:10). We ought

2. James Stalker, *The Preacher and His Models* (New York: Hodder and Stoughton, 1891), 167.

to bedeck the gospel we proclaim with the moral beauty of personal holiness in Christ. Our blamelessness ought likewise to adorn our criticism of others. Few things are worse than a hypocritical critic. If our people sense that there is compromise in our lives, our criticism of them, no matter how sincere and legitimate, will most likely fall on deaf ears. Beware of seeking to deal with the speck in your brother's eye all the while having a log protruding from your own (see Matt. 7:3–5).

Does your life epitomize the very flaw you are critiquing? Is there known compromise in your life? Is there undealt with sin you have committed that has marred your reputation before your people?

As a clean conscience is necessary to rightly receive criticism, so it is needed to rightly give criticism. If your people would hear your rebuke, they must sense it is coming from one who needs no rebuke. This is why Paul stresses that an elder must be of good report, even among those outside of the church (see 1 Tim. 3:7). The apostle is not calling us to sinless perfection, but to a lifestyle that is "above reproach" in every sphere (1 Tim. 3:2 ESV). John Brown writes, "If a teacher of Christianity be regarded by his people with reverence and love, as really 'honest in the sacred cause,' firmly believing every statement he makes, exemplifying in his own character and conduct every virtue and duty he recommends, truly desirous of promoting their spiritual improvement and ultimate salvation, truth from his lips is likely to prevail with double sway, attention will be readily yielded, and conviction, instead of being resisted, will be welcomed, and obedience cheerfully rendered."[3]

Our people are always watching us. It only takes one public sin to lose their confidence, but it takes many years of integrity

---

3. John Brown, *An Exposition of the Epistle of Paul to the Galatians* (Edinburgh: The Banner of Truth Trust, 2001), 205.

to gain it. If we would have their ears when the time comes to criticize them, our ministry must be pervaded with the ethos of long-term holiness.

A Relational Ministry

Isolation is a real danger in pastoral ministry. Some church cultures actually encourage this, elevating the pastor above the rest of the congregation and making him next to unapproachable. But if we would effectively criticize our people, we must be actively involved in their lives. We must have genuine relationships with them. We must know them. David Dickson says of the elder, "He must be acquainted with them all, old and young, their history, their occupations, their habits, their ways of thinking. They and their children should be their personal friends, so that they naturally turn to him as the one on whom they can depend as a kind and sympathizing friend and a faithful counselor."[4]

Of course, this kind of closeness to our sheep will not happen in a day, but takes much time and self-sacrifice. Pastors have the great privilege of being invited into the sweetest joys and the most heartbreaking sorrows our church members experience. We are there when babies are born. We are there when babies die. We are there to officiate their weddings and to walk with them through cancer and the shadow of death. And we get to journey with our people through the mundaneness of everyday life in between. We need to seize upon these moments to get into the lives of our people, showing them our care and seeking to cultivate genuine and deep relationships with them. Where such relationship is lacking, criticism will ordinarily not be well taken. But when we have the ethos of a friend, they will gladly hear us.

---

4. David Dickson, *The Elder and His Work* (repr., Dallas: Presbyterian Heritage Publications, 1990), 15.

An Affirming Ministry

Our people need to have a deep sense that we are on their side. If they perceive us as faultfinders rather than encouragers, we have failed. The pastor must criticize when necessary, but he is not a resident critic. Our ministries ought to be suffused with positive affirmation of our people. Without it, our attempts to correct or rebuke them will be in vain. Sam Crabtree encourages us, "Behave in such a consistently affirming way that when correction must be made, there is no mistake in the recipient's mind that you are for him and not against him."[5] The ministry is full of opportunities for this; we just need eyes to see them.

- Keep your eyes open for all the little, often unnoticed ways your congregants serve the church. Take the time to call or write a card thanking and encouraging them in their work.[6] When appropriate, publicly affirm them for their service.
- Keep your eyes open for signs of growth and transformation in the lives of your people. Where you see real spiritual change, even if it be minor, make sure to verbally affirm it.
- Keep your eyes open for those who are particularly downcast and tempted to despair. Meet them in their darkness and spur them on with encouraging words concerning the ways you see God's grace at work in their lives and circumstances.
- Keep your eyes open for ways your congregants can help you. When you have a decision to make, seek out their advice. When you have a particular need that corresponds

5. Sam Crabtree, *Practicing Affirmation: God-Centered Praise of Those Who Are Not God* (Wheaton, IL: Crossway, 2011), 144–45.
6. If possible, avoid doing this by email as it is not as personal and meaningful. That being said, an email is better than nothing.

to their expertise, ask for help. These kinds of requests go a long way in affirming the value of our people.

Later in this chapter we will discuss the role of affirmation in the act of criticism, but the point here is that your ministry should be one of regular encouragement and occasional critique, not regular critique and occasional encouragement. The ethos of affirmation will promote receptivity to criticism.

THE PATHOS OF CRITICISM

We turn now to the nature of our critique. In all of our criticism we must aim at the hearts of our people. This is what Aristotle referred to as *pathos*. We reach the ears of those we criticize through their affections. But how do we get to their hearts?

Exude Compassion

First, by giving them our own hearts. If we would engage the affections of our people, we must be affectionate toward them in our confrontation. We should be able to say with the apostle, "O ye Corinthians, our mouth is open unto you, our heart is enlarged" (2 Cor. 6:11). Nothing will open the hearts of our people to us like our hearts being manifestly open to them. "When the people see that you unfeignedly love them," explains Richard Baxter, "they will hear any thing and bear any thing from you."[7] By our word choice, tone of voice, facial expressions, and other body language, we should seek to communicate compassion and genuine care.

We are exhorted in Galatians 6:1, "Brethren, if a man be overtaken in a fault, ye which are spiritual, restore such an one in

---

7. Richard Baxter, *The Reformed Pastor* (Edinburgh: The Banner of Truth Trust, 1974), 118.

the spirit of meekness." The word translated "meekness" means "forbearing, large-hearted, gentle, courteous, considerate, generous, lenient, moderate. In summary, it is describing a quality that is the opposite of irritability, rudeness, and abrasiveness."[8] If we would have the hearts of our people in criticism, we must be governed by such a spirit of humble love. The thirty-first resolution of Jonathan Edwards is a helpful and convicting guide at this point: "*Resolved*, Never to say anything at all against any body, but when it is perfectly agreeable to the highest degree of Christian honor, and of love to mankind, agreeable to the lowest humility, and sense of my own faults and failings, and agreeable to the golden rule; often, when I have said anything against any one, to bring it to, and try it strictly by, the test of this Resolution."[9]

Is there any question in the minds of your people that you love them? What is your verbal and nonverbal communication saying about the disposition of your heart? Do you genuinely love them? Are you seeking their eternal welfare in your critique?[10]

Encompass with Affirmation

We reach their heart, second, by our affirmation. Constructive criticism is best carried out in the context of a ministry of encouragement. But it is also the case that effective critique ought ordinarily to be immediately preceded and followed by

8. Wayne Mack, *A Homework Manual for Biblical Counseling: Personal and Interpersonal Problems* (Phillipsburg, NJ: P&R, 1979), 12.

9. See Sereno E. Dwight, *Memoirs of Jonathan Edwards* in *The Works of Jonathan Edwards* (repr.; Edinburgh: Banner of Truth Trust, 1974), 1:xxi.

10. Sam Crabtree provides the following helpful questions: "When you correct, whose agenda are you following? Are your corrections driven by your own preferences, your own disappointments and frustrations? Or are your corrections driven by what God desires for each person? Would other godly people confirm the God-centeredness of your corrections and the authenticity of the love that is motivating you?" (*Practicing Affirmation*, 147).

encouragement.[11] This has often been called the "sandwich principle." If we criticize people without affirming them in any way
before or after, they will likely receive the criticism as a reflection
of their entire personality. In our rebuking, we want people to
hear us saying, "I am affirming you as a person and appreciate
you, but I do have a concern."

Let's say you have a young mother with a rambunctious little boy. He has been consistently yelling and recently created a
scene during Lord's Day worship services. The issue needs to
be addressed, but how? In order to make a point, you could get
straight to the criticism, not pulling any punches: "Little Johnny
has been incredibly noisy during worship services over the past
month. Do you realize how distracting this is to everyone else?
You either need to keep him under control or take him outside."
Such a critique may produce pathos in this mother, but not the
kind you want! Far better and more Christlike to sandwich the
criticism between affirmation, like so:

- *Preceding Affirmation:* "Carol, I have been so encouraged
  to see the way you are seeking to raise Johnny to know and
  love the Lord, especially your commitment to bring him
  to public worship every Lord's Day and to nurture him in
  God's truth."
- *Criticism:* "But I have noticed the last few weeks that he
  has been quite loud during worship services. I am concerned that it might be distracting others from hearing the
  Word."
- *Subsequent Affirmation:* "I know you value the importance
  of children worshiping with their families, and that is a

11. There are exceptions to this, of course. Sometimes it is necessary to get
straight to a rebuke in order to make a point (see, for example, Matt. 23:13–
36; Gal. 1:6–9). Paul's example with the wayward church in Corinth, however,
is a great example of the role of affirmation in rebuke (see 1 Cor. 1:4–9).

great and God-honoring thing! But perhaps the next time he starts getting noisy during the service, you could take him out."

What a difference it makes when criticism is sandwiched between affirmations! Of course, the affirmations need to be sincere. Don't affirm someone in a way that is not true to their person or true to your convictions. But when sincere affirmation encompasses our criticism, it will go a long way toward reducing defensiveness and gaining the hearts of those we critique.[12]

Emphasize the Consequences

Third, sanctified pathos comes about by helping our people see the consequences of their errors. Our sinful beliefs and actions are never without repercussions. Helping people to grasp those repercussions can go a long way toward using our criticism for their growth.

If there is a man in your congregation pursuing the American dream to the neglect of his family, don't just call him out on it. Don't merely show him his sin in the light of God's Word; seek to impress upon him the consequences of his behavior. The negative repercussions are vast, but focus on those that you believe will bear the most weight in his conscience. It may be helpful to put it in the form of a question. For example, what message is he communicating to his children by his unbiblical actions? Here are a few possibilities:

- Daddy's work is more important than me.
- Riches are more important than relationships.

12. Notice how Paul also uses the sandwich principle of constructive criticism in epistles such as 1 Corinthians, bookending them with affirmations, and then focusing in the center of the book on various criticisms and their solutions.

- The more money I have, the happier I will be.
- My self-worth is no greater than my earthly success and prosperity.

No Christian father wants his children to believe these things. But often we don't realize the devastating repercussions of our actions. Bringing them to light is an important way to open the hearts of our people to our rebukes and lead to lasting change.

Express Hope

Finally, we reach our people's affections by giving them hope. Criticism is largely the application of God's law. We wield the precepts of God, which are either explicitly revealed or deduced by good and necessary consequence, in order to expose sin. But we must take care not to do so without also setting forth the hope of the gospel. If our people get the sense from us that they are a lost cause, their hearts will not be open to us. Constructive criticism necessitates a measure of biblical optimism. If there is no hope of change, then there is nothing constructive about our criticism.

As pastors, we must beware of Christless criticism. When critiquing our sheep, we need to point them to the grace of God in Christ that is efficacious to cleanse them of their guilt and to empower them to put sin to death. When rebuking one whom we suspect is not a genuine believer, we need to call them to look to Christ for justifying righteousness and sanctifying holiness. Whatever their condition and however serious the sin that we are criticizing, we must not fail to tell people of the hope freely offered them in the gospel. Ask yourself, *Is my criticism seeking to lead people to Christ?* If the hearts of our people belong to Christ, their hearts will be opened by the proclamation of Christ.[13]

13. To the contrary, proclaiming Christ in our criticism could also lead to antipathy if the one we are critiquing is not a Christian. But the call is still the

THE LOGOS OF CRITICISM

Without possessing personal holiness (ethos) and the hearts of our people (pathos), the most carefully constructed argument will get us nowhere. This, however, does not in any way downplay the significance of logos when giving critique. The content of our criticism is very important and needs to be carefully worded and grounded.

Carefully Worded

It doesn't matter what we say only, but how we say it. Word choice is a critical element of constructive criticism. While certain sheep may need a sharp word that is straight and to the point, ordinarily it is best to choose words that are clothed with the gentleness and kindness of the Spirit. Charles Wingard writes, "When you must speak to a problem or express a concern, measure in advance the effects of your words. If you prize a reputation for being direct, think again. A tell-it-like-it-is attitude won't do. Mature leaders think carefully about how their words will be received. When dealing with controversy, bluntness is most often harmful. Be truthful, but don't state your position in a way that provokes hurt feelings or an angry and defensive response."[14]

We need to wisely consider which words will be most likely to evoke the response we are seeking. For example, you have a young man in the congregation who has been particularly distracted during your preaching as of late. What is the cause of his distraction? A beautiful young woman. For numerous weeks

---

same: to set before them the hope that is alone found in Christ, praying that the Spirit would give them new hearts through the gospel. There is nothing more loving that we can do.

14. Charles Malcom Wingard, *Help for the New Pastor: Practical Advice for Your First Year of Ministry* (Phillipsburg, NJ: P&R, 2018), 88.

you have noticed him whispering in her ear throughout your messages. He gives every appearance that he is more preoccupied with her than with the truth of God's Word. How will you respond?

You could give him a scolding rebuke, but it is far better to choose gracious words when confronting this young man: "Charlie, I've noticed lately that you and Kate have been developing a relationship, and I'm excited to see that happening. I pray that God—if it is His will—will greatly bless your relationship. Romance is truly a biblical and beautiful thing as long as it is confined within proper, biblical parameters. I just have one area of concern that I would like to raise briefly with you. It seems to me that you have been a bit distracted lately when sitting with Kate in church. I'm afraid that when you whisper quite frequently during the sermon that you are not able to take in the full message God is bringing you. So I would like you to make a real effort from here on in to avoid whispering together during the sermon, but rather to try to take in as much of the sermon as possible and then talk about it and pray over it after the worship service is completed. I hope you will follow my advice. I am thrilled that you seem to have a growing relationship with Kate, and I pray that God will bless your relationship abundantly." Rather than crushing the young man with hard words, it is far better to provide a warm, fatherly admonition.

It is also important to choose words that do not exaggerate the problem. In the desire to get our point across we may be tempted to use stronger language than actually fits the situation: "Charlie, you haven't listened to a word I have said from the pulpit for weeks. You have been giving your undivided attention to Kate." Though we may think that such extreme language will be effective in getting our point across, it will actually backfire on us. Exaggerated remarks undermine our critique (along with our integrity!) and will lead to Charlie getting defensive. Let us take care to choose words that befit the issue being addressed and beware of exaggeration.

Carefully Grounded

Effective criticism must be built on a solid foundation. We must take care to carefully study the situation and the Scriptures if our critique would not be groundless.

First, we need to ground our critique on concrete and sufficient evidence. We have all been the objects of criticism that was built on the sands of assumptions or unreliable sources. Ask yourself the following questions:

- *Are there any assumptions you are making about the person's character or intentions that are potentially skewing your perspective?* For the sake of making a point, let's say this young woman who Charlie is distractedly fixated on is your daughter. Might there be protective, paternal suppositions concerning this young man that color the situation darker than it really is?
- *Have you witnessed the problem for yourself?* If not, are you basing your critique on reliable sources? In this instance you yourself have witnessed Charlie's distracted fixation, but if it was instead relayed to you by a congregant, you would want to carefully weigh who it was coming from, as well as the number of witnesses.
- *Is the situation serious or persistent enough to warrant criticism?* If Charlie whispered into Kate's ear one time during one of your sermons, then such a confrontation would be utterly groundless. We mustn't be hasty in jumping to conclusions without sufficient cause for concern.

Second, we need to ground our critique on the Scriptures. Too often criticism is founded on subjective opinions or biases.

It is the God-breathed Word that makes the man of God fit for every rebuke and criticism (see 2 Tim. 3:16–17). Does God's Word speak clearly on this issue? Does His Word deem this important enough to address?[15]

Charlie needs to understand that your criticism is not founded on some power-hungry desire to have his undivided attention when preaching. This is not about you; it is about Charlie and God. If there would be true contrition and genuine change, we must impress upon this young man's conscience the precepts of God's Word and show him how his behavior does not appear to be aligning with it.

- *James 1:21:* The Scriptures teach the vital necessity of a careful listening and faith-filled reception of the Word.
- *Hebrews 2:1:* The Scriptures warn of the disastrous consequences of failing to pay attention to the Word.

If possible, ground your criticism in a passage or truth of God's Word that is most relevant to your critique. Help the one you are criticizing to see that you are not giving them your own personal, subjective opinions, but that your concerns are founded on the Word of God.

EYEING CHRIST AS YOU CRITICIZE

As we seek to use criticism to lovingly care for our people, it is inevitable that we will fail. There will be times when our attempts will be deficient in ethos, pathos, and logos. Even our best attempts will be fraught with imperfection.

15. Sam Crabtree provides a helpful chart to help discern when to criticize, arguing that we ought only to criticize when we are convinced our position is right and when we are convinced it is an important enough matter to warrant addressing (see *Practicing Affirmation,* 161–63). These convictions, of course,

How we continually stand in need of the gospel! Consider how perfectly this triad of sanctified critique was displayed in the earthly life of our Savior. His incarnate humanity was clothed in the ethos of holiness. He was a man with perfectly engaged affections, always aiming at the pathos of his listeners. And his logos was flawless, possessing a word choice and biblical logic that comforted His weakest followers and shut the mouths of His greatest foes. Behold your righteousness in Him! And behold in Christ the one through whom you can be strengthened for the important and necessary task of criticism. Left to our own resources, none of us are sufficient for these things. But by the power of His Spirit, we can criticize constructively to the glory of God and the good of our hearers.

---

must be founded on the Word of God.

8

CULTIVATING A CHURCH CULTURE OPEN TO CONSTRUCTIVE CRITIQUE

The temptation when examining the subject of criticism is to think in exclusively individualistic terms. How do *I* receive criticism? How do *I* give criticism? These are important questions that have occupied our attention up to this point. But the stress of biblical ecclesiology is on the corporate and the communal. No Christian is an island. We are members of one body with Christ as the head. This requires us to ask the question, How should the church relate to criticism?

There are two equally dangerous extremes that local congregations may fall into as they relate to criticism. The first is a culture of criticism where nearly everything and everyone is viewed with suspicion and negativity. Self-righteous criticism becomes the defining character trait of the church. The second is an uncritical culture where no one dares ask questions or utter a word of critique, especially toward the leadership. It is not that the people aren't critical; they are. They just can't conceive of making their negative judgments known through proper biblical and church channels (see Matt. 18:15–17).

Your church probably falls somewhere between these two extremes, but still may have the tendency to veer off into one error or the other. A healthy church culture is one where verbal critique is neither dominant nor absent. Garrett Kell sums this up well: "What we don't want to do is create a culture of critics who are constantly eyeing one another for mistakes. But what we do want to see is a church deepen in their love and care for one another so much that they are willing to engage in deep, painful, graceful, helpful, character-shaping conversations that will bring God much glory."[1] Is not this culture of loving critique a wonderful aspiration to have for your congregation? When the church rightly relates to criticism, it brings great glory to God and great good to man. In this chapter we will examine some ways to cultivate such a culture among our people.

PREACH CHRIST

A healthy church is one that is shaped by the gospel. Our people need to see the beauty of Christ. Nothing will enable them to lovingly and humbly give and receive constructive critique more than heart-searching, expository gospel preaching. This is our great task and privilege as ministers—to proclaim Christ. And as we do, whether we recognize it or not, we will be promoting a healthy culture of criticism.

What is it that fuels both a hypercritical spirit and an aversion to criticism? It is a high view of self. Man criticizes incessantly in order to feel better about self. Man runs from or suppresses criticism directed his way for the same purpose, to protect and promote the self. There is a certain high-mindedness native to

1. Garrett Kell, "Giving and Receiving Godly Criticism: Sharpening Each Other with Your Words," 9 Marks, February 3, 2015, https://www.9marks .org/article/giving-and-receiving-godly-criticism-sharpening-each-other -with-your-words/.

us all that is averse to both giving and receiving constructive critique.

At the cross, however, man's high-mindedness is utterly decimated as he comes face-to-face with the savage heinousness of sin. Sin is insurrection of the highest sort, a rebellious uprising against the Creator and Ruler of all things. While the law certainly does much to show us our sin, it is actually the gospel that gives us the most alarming impression of the infinite affront that our sin is to God. David Wells writes, "The biblical gospel asserts . . . that the self is twisted, that it is maladjusted in its relationship to God and others, that it is full of deceit and rationalizations, that it is lawless, that it is in rebellion, and indeed one must die to self in order to live."[2] The hamartiology of the gospel shatters the exalted self-perceptions of our congregants, as well as our own.

Who can behold the Son of God being submerged under the floodwaters of divine judgment, utterly forsaken by His Father, and think nothing of this? Alfred Poirier, in his excellent article entitled "The Cross and Criticism," explains, "In response to my sin, the cross has criticized and judged me more intensely, deeply, pervasively, and truly than anyone else ever could."[3] To hear the proclamation of Christ crucified is to hear the most comprehensive and cutting critique of ourselves. In the light of the cross, we are taught the painful but liberating truth that we are always worse than our worst human critic makes us out to be. It is not possible to paint us too blackly.

The breathtaking reality is that at the cross Christ has swallowed up the judgment that our rebellion deserved. In Him, God views us as though we have not the slightest taint of sin.

2. David Wells, *No Place for Truth* (Grand Rapids: Eerdmans, 1993), 179.
3. Alfred J. Poirier, "The Cross and Criticism," *The Journal of Biblical Counseling* 17.3 (1999): 18.

He justifies us! If our congregations really understood this, they would exclaim, "If God justifies me, accepts me, and will never forsake me, then why should I feel insecure and fear criticism?"[4] Such is a practical outworking of the gospel. To the extent that our churches possess an experiential acquaintance of their gracious acceptance, adopted status, and unshakeable security in Jesus Christ, they will not excessively fear the frowns of man or be quick to issue hypercritical frowns toward others.

This is the kind of culture of criticism our churches need— one in which the cross looms large and men, women, boys, and girls see themselves as crucified with Christ. The gospel humbles us lower than the most scathing human criticism, but it simultaneously exalts us into God's gracious favor so that the negative appraisal of our fellow man no longer devastates us.

PRAY CONTINUOUSLY

The New Testament everywhere emphasizes the primacy of preaching. There is no means more used by God to etch the image of Christ in His people than the proclamation of the Scriptures. But faithful preaching must always be married to fervent praying. Ian Hamilton writes that it is the prayer closet that "most manifests our conviction that God the Holy Spirit is the great convincer, convicter, and applier of Christ's saving merits to sinners."[5] We can preach Christ with the greatest passion, the most eloquent rhetoric, and the most convincing logic, but if we are depending on our own abilities it is all in vain. The apostles devoted themselves to prayer and the ministry of the Word (see Acts 6:4). We must do the same if we would see our preaching

---

4. Poirier, 19.
5. Ian Hamilton, *What Is Experiential Calvinism?* (Grand Rapids: Reformation Heritage Books, 2015), 19–20.

of the cross bear the fruit of humility and love necessary for a church culture of healthy critique.

The apostle Paul is exemplary here. He was not a man who preached frequently and prayed occasionally. Listen to his testimony:

> I thank my God *always* on your behalf, for the grace of God which is given you by Jesus Christ. (1 Cor. 1:4)

> *Cease not* to give thanks for you, making mention of you in my prayers. (Eph. 1:16)

> For this cause we also, since the day we heard it, *do not cease* to pray for you. (Col. 1:9)

> We give thanks to God *always* for you all, making mention of you in our prayers. (1 Thess. 1:2)

> *Night and day* praying exceedingly that we might see your face, and might perfect that which is lacking in your faith. (1 Thess. 3:10)

> Wherefore also we pray *always* for you . . . (2 Thess. 1:11)

> . . . *without ceasing* I have remembrance of thee in my prayers *night and day*. (2 Tim. 1:3)

Paul was always praying night and day without ceasing for the churches. Can the same be said of us? There is no magic formula to creating a healthy culture of constructive critique in your congregation. No man-made techniques will do. Only God can bring about such a culture. It is the work of the Spirit to create and grow a God-fearing humility and self-forgetting love in the hearts of Christians. Thus, we must devote ourselves to prayer just as fervently as we do to the ministry of the Word. We must be men of ceaseless prayer for our congregations.

What should we be praying for? Again, Paul is of great help to us. We ought to pray that our people may be rooted and grounded in the love of Christ (see Eph. 3:14–21) so that by His power they might "increase and abound in love one toward another" (1 Thess. 3:12; see also Phil. 1:9). The apostle, writes John Stott, "is convinced, as we must be, that only divine power can generate divine love in the divine society."[6] And so we find him on his knees, praying for the super-abounding power of the Spirit who alone can open hearts to the incomprehensible love of Christ. It is only as we are gripped by the love of Christ for us that our lives will abound in love toward God and others. "Our speech, our thoughts, our actions, our reactions, our relationships, our goals, our values," argues D. A. Carson, "all are transformed if only we live in the self-conscious enjoyment of the love of Christ."[7] This is what our people need. To be continuously transformed by love so that they in turn can continuously love.

It is Spirit-wrought love that will deliver us from a hypercritical spirit. It will keep our churches from possessing a nitpicky culture of faultfinding. For love, as Paul tells us, "beareth all things, believeth all things, hopeth all things, endureth all things" (1 Cor. 13:7). It does not assume the worst, but the best. It frees men and women from their incessant self-preoccupation so that they can genuinely care for others and constructively critique others. Pray for such divine love to pervade your congregation. Pray for it night and day.

6. John R. W. Stott, "Paul Prays for the Church," *Themelios* 2.1 (1976): 4.
7. D. A. Carson, *Praying with Paul: A Call to Spiritual Reformation*, 2nd ed. (Grand Rapids, Baker Academic, 2014), 175.

PLEAD GUILTY

Pastors are sinners. This may seem like a painfully obvious point, but many pastors feel they cannot be open about their struggle with indwelling sin. Even when confronted with sin, they refuse to admit and confess it. Few things could be more detrimental to the church. What is needed is a ministry suffused with "the godly attitude of a broken man ministering to broken men."[8] When a pastor owns his failures, it gives his congregation the freedom to admit their own. There are times when we must plead guilty.

Recently, I (Nick) made a significant overstatement in preaching. What I had intended to say was perfectly sound, but what actually came out of my mouth was extreme, lacking pastoral sensitivity, and confusing. In the passion of the moment I did not recognize it, nor did anyone express concern after the fact. The following morning, however, as I reviewed the Lord's Day, I was sorely convicted about it. So before I began my morning sermon the following Sunday, I confessed to the congregation that I had failed to speak rightly, clarified what I meant to say, and asked for their forgiveness. It was very simple, really. I pled guilty.

Given the public nature of the ministry and the fact that we continue to be sinners, we have many opportunities like this to confess our sins to our people. Of course, this could be overdone. Our people don't need a laundry list of our daily sins. We must exercise wisdom here. But when we have sinned against a specific congregant, we should be quick to confess and ask for forgiveness. And when we commit a public sin before the whole church, we should not wait for their rebuke to confess it, but express our contrition and make it right as soon as possible. The

---

8. Peter A. Lillback, *Saint Peter's Principles: Leadership for Those Who Already Know Their Incompetence* (Phillipsburg, NJ: P&R, 2019), 360.

temptation might be to think that if we do so we will lose the respect of our people. This may be the case in certain instances, but ordinarily our humble confession will win us our people's admiration and will serve to encourage them to be honest about their sin struggles.

We are broken men ministering to broken men and women. Our people need to see this. Don't put on a façade and pretend that you have it all together. Don't give the false appearance of having a picture-perfect family. Don't act like you have all the answers. Acknowledge your weaknesses and be vulnerable before your people. It will go a long way in promoting a wholesome culture of constructive critique in your church.

PROVIDE PLATFORMS OR CONTEXTS

It is also important to provide platforms for our people to voice their concerns. We ought not to have a neutral attitude toward constructive critique, merely taking it if and when it comes. We should be inviting it! Our people should sense that we are eager and desirous to be challenged by them and learn from them because we are deeply conscious of the fact that we do not have it all figured out. We have not arrived, and therefore we will take all the help we can get.

This must begin at the level of the church's leadership. As the eldership goes, so goes the church. Seek to cultivate strong relationships with your elders—relationships in which there is a healthy vulnerability and transparency. Don't be afraid to express your weaknesses and struggles to them. Don't shrink back from asking them for prayer. Let them know that you need them and that you welcome their feedback.

Once or twice a year, consider setting aside some time during a regular elders' meeting to discuss your preaching. Ask them to give an honest evaluation of your sermons, and humbly request any concerns they might have. It is wise to provide some clear guidance. Few of these men have taken a course in Reformed homiletics; what should they look for in faithful preaching of the Word? Ask them specific questions, and give them the questions ahead of time for reflection. Of course, make clear that this is a time for *constructive* criticism, not a time to bash the pastor or ride their particular hobby horse. When a congregant critiques your sermon and you find it difficult to discern how valid their concern is, take it before your elders and seek their judgment on the matter. Let your elders know that you genuinely desire to grow as a preacher and that you believe they can be of real assistance to you here.

It is also good to have meetings where you discuss with your elders the overall health of the congregation. Don't downplay the positive fruit and evident grace manifest in the church, but establish a platform once or twice a year to talk about specific weaknesses and areas where growth is needed. An annual elders' retreat is a great way to accomplish this. Be honest about the condition of the church. Praise God for the strengths you see and lament the weaknesses. Then discuss and plan how to overcome those weaknesses by God's grace.

Seek to instill in your elders a holy restlessness. Don't be duped as an eldership into thinking your congregation is beyond the bounds of just critique. When the members of your church see their leadership owning their weaknesses and seeking change, they will be encouraged to do the same in their own lives.

From time to time address the subject of criticism from the pulpit. As was briefly demonstrated in the opening chapters, the Bible is not unacquainted with criticism of every sort. When you come to these texts or are addressing subjects like gossip or pride, seize upon the opportunity to train your people in giving and receiving healthy criticism. Consider possibly teaching a class on the subject. It is a very relevant issue that every person in your congregation deals with. Make it clear to your people not only what biblical critique looks like, but that you are open to theirs. Nothing will serve more to open their hearts to yours.

PLAN BIG

A church with a culture of healthy criticism is a church that is not afraid to fail. It is a church that has been delivered from the bondage of perfectionism. As shepherds, we need to have a vision that reaches beyond our own abilities and resources. We need to plan big. If our vision for the church does not leave room for potential failure, then it is too small. Craig Hamilton writes, "If you can always jump over the bar it's because it's too low. If a person hits 100% of their goals and plans, that's probably a good indicator that they're playing it safe."[9] If you play it safe as a church leader, you are unknowingly fostering a church culture that is averse to criticism.

What will your people think of you if, after recognizing the church is deficient in evangelistic outreach, you develop a plan to reach the community and it utterly fails? They will most likely criticize. But is it not worth the risk? Is it not incumbent on you as a pastor to seek to turn your congregation outward in evangelism? And is it not better to fail trying than not to try at all?

Our people need to see that we are not afraid of failing in our endeavors for Christ. If we live in the fear of failure, it is most likely because we fear criticism. We want to appear successful. We don't want our congregants or fellow ministers to see our weaknesses. But the reality is that we need failure—and so do our churches. Failure is an important component of spiritual maturation. It grounds us in reality. It humbles us, reminding us of our

9. Craig Hamilton, *Wisdom in Leadership: The How and Why of Leading the People You Serve* (Sydney: Matthias Media, 2015), 217.

weakness and our need of Christ. And it delivers our churches from being insulated in a mirage of self-conceit. A church that is not afraid to fail is usually a church that is not afraid of criticism. So plan big, knowing that God will use even your failures to adorn the church with humble Christlikeness.

CULTIVATE PATIENCE

As you preach Christ, pray continuously, plead guilty, provide platforms, and plan big, you must look with great expectation for God's work in your congregation. Patience will be needed. A culture open to constructive critique will not transpire overnight. But the others-oriented love and care that marks such a community is worth striving after with all of your might for all your days.

PART 4

THEOLOGICAL VISION FOR COPING WITH CRITICISM

9

REORIENT YOUR PERSPECTIVE

Imagine an elderly friend of yours is given a copy of this book. He is able to flip through its crisp pages and to discern the presence of many words, but because of his weak vision he cannot actually read it until he puts on his glasses. Suddenly, through the assistance of optical lenses, he is able to see the book as it really is and to profit from its content. This illustration is used by Calvin to explain how the Scriptures function in our lives. They are "spectacles" that enable us with our sin-clouded sight to see the world, ourselves, and God truly. Without these lenses, we continue in a world that everywhere reveals the glory of God, but we do not have eyes to see it. We are like blind men standing before the sun. When, however, we put these glasses on by faith, we see rightly and clearly.[1]

As pastors we are prone to be like hazy-eyed old men when hit with verbal flak, having flawed perceptions of our critics and their words. But God in His rich grace has provided us with divinely inspired lenses that can renew our vision and enable us to see what matters most. Under the blessing of the Spirit,

---

1. John Calvin, *Institutes of the Christian Religion*, trans. Ford Lewis Battles, ed. John T. McNeill (Philadelphia: Westminster Press, 1960), 1.6.2.

the Scriptures lift our gaze from our present hostility to behold larger-than-life truths. These God-breathed bifocals shift our focus away from ourselves to God, His church, judgment day, and eternity. With these truths enveloping our sight, criticism is put in its rightful place. The apostle Paul has much to teach us about such a reformation of perspective. Thus, we conclude our book by focusing largely on his ministerial vision.

A GOD-GLORIFYING VISION

The chief end of our ministry is the promotion of the glory of God. We cannot remind ourselves too often that the ministry is not about us! Paul wrote that his apostolic ministry was "for the sake of [Christ's] name" (Rom. 1:5 ESV). In what he knew would be his last address to the elders of the church at Ephesus, he confessed, "But none of these things [referring to the suffering he would endure for the gospel] move me, neither count I my life dear unto myself, so that I might finish my course with joy, and the ministry, which I have received of the Lord Jesus, to testify the gospel of the grace of God" (Acts 20:24). Verbal and physical opposition did not move Paul. He wasn't shaken by it. Why? Because he did not prize his own life. The apostle understood that he was a servant of Christ, a man who had been entrusted with a massive stewardship from his Master, and he was consumed with a passion to faithfully carry out that stewardship with joy.

Undergirding this pursuit of the exaltation of Christ's name was a deep, intimate acquaintance with Christ. Paul was no neophyte in the school of communion with the Triune God. He was a man who feared God. John Murray describes the soul that fears God as one in which "God is constantly in the center of our thought and apprehension, and life is characterized by the all-pervasive consciousness of dependence upon him and responsibility to him."[2] Is God continually at the forefront of our vision? Do we know this "all-pervasive consciousness of dependence upon [God] and responsibility to him"?

Such was the soul of the apostle. He was consumed with a vision of the glory of God. He recognized that he was utterly dependent on God and had a profound responsibility to God. His Triune Lord was at the center of everything he did. Such a fear of God, writes John Flavel, "devours carnal fears."[3] Paul's vision of Jesus Christ in His divine beauty and strength swallowed up the fear of man. He was liberated from the idol of self; he was freed from the bondage of man's applause and approval. He could face great opposition because he had a controlling sense that his life and ministry were not about him.

Paul found his joy in the exaltation of Jesus Christ, and he was willing to suffer the greatest hostility to see it come to pass. Writing to the church at Philippi, he expressed his delight over the way the gospel was advancing through his imprisonment (see Phil. 1:12–14). God had raised up many men who were boldly preaching Christ, and the gospel was going forth mightily. Some of these preachers, however, had bad intentions toward Paul in their preaching, seeking to exalt themselves and publicly shame the apostle (see v. 16). We don't know the exact nature of what was happening here, but it is clear that Paul rejoiced even in these ill-willed preachers. Why? Because Christ was being proclaimed (see v. 18)! One commentator explains, "As long as Christ is preached, Paul is unconcerned about his own position or fame in comparison to that of other preachers. So those who intended to cause Paul harm by exalting themselves above him

2. John Murray, *The Epistle to the Romans,* New International Commentary on the New Testament (Grand Rapids: Eerdmans, 1965), 1:105.

3. John Flavel, *A Practical Treatise on Fear: Its Varieties, Uses, Causes, Effects and Remedies,* in *The Works of John Flavel* (repr., Edinburgh: Banner of Truth Trust, 1968), 3:252.

as preachers of Christ actually caused him to rejoice because Christ was preached. . . . The advancement of the message, not the advancement of Paul, is the source of Paul's joy."[4]

What convicting words! It was not personal advancement, but gospel advancement that fueled the apostle's joy. He could rejoice in the ministries of those who were against him so long as they were for Christ. Can such be said of us? Has our vision been lifted beyond our minuscule selves to the majestic splendor of the Savior of the world? Has the fear of God engulfed our preoccupation with what man thinks of us?

Brother, strive in dependence on the Spirit to daily seek after a more expansive vision of God's mind-renewing glory in His Word. Pray that God would cause you to be ablaze with a passion for the exaltation of Jesus Christ. Strive to cultivate this zeal for God in His divine splendor. Such will bring the critical words and harmful intentions of men into proper perspective.

A CHURCH-BUILDING VISION

A God-glorifying vision is always wedded to a church-building vision because it is through the strengthening and expansion of the church that God is most exalted in the world. What John Piper declares to be the end of Christian preaching applies to every facet of the Christian ministry: "The purpose is that God's infinite worth and beauty be exalted in the everlasting, white-hot worship of the blood-bought bride of Christ from every people, language, tribe, and nation."[5] As pastors, we have a God-ordained commission to promote the Spirit-wrought worship of God, but such worship always happens in the context

4. G. Walter Hansen, *The Letter to the Philippians,* Pillar New Testament Commentary, ed. D. A. Carson (Grand Rapids: Eerdmans, 2009), 75.

5. John Piper, *Expository Exultation: Christian Preaching as Worship* (Wheaton, IL: Crossway, 2018), 21.

of the church. It is "the blood-bought bride of Christ" who is rendering God the glory due His name. And this should be our absorbing preoccupation.

The ministry is not about us; it is about the spiritual well-being of Christ's church. This is easy to affirm, but if God were to lay bare the inner recesses of our souls, we might be surprised at how woefully little of this we know in our experience. Lewis Allen expresses some of the chief aims that fuel the average pastor: "Job satisfaction, influence, intellectual stimulation, personal gratification, a quiet life (or a noisy, hectic life), peer group approval, or congregational applause."[6] If you are anything like us, some of these motivations have at least the potential to drive your ministerial labors more than they should. Such a vision never rises above I, myself, and me.

Again, the apostle shows us a better way. Though Paul suffered greatly for the well-being of the church at Corinth, they had become his hostile critics through the influence of false teachers. Second Corinthians is his astonishing response to this unfavorable situation.[7] He writes, "And I will very gladly spend and be spent for you; though the more abundantly I love you, the less I be loved" (2 Cor. 12:15). Even if lavishing love on the Corinthians meant that he would be loved less by them, he would continue to pour himself out on their behalf. Think about that. If as you pour yourself out in self-giving love, people grow more and more to despise you, would you continue to love nonetheless? How could Paul say this? His chief concern was the well-being of their souls. It was not a quiet life, applause and approval,

6. Lewis Allen, *The Preacher's Catechism* (Wheaton, IL: Crossway, 2018), 120.

7. For a fuller treatment of 2 Corinthians with specific application to facing criticism in the pastoral ministry see John MacArthur's insightful lecture, T4G, "Criticism: A Pastor's All-too-Common Experience," 2018 seminar, https://t4g.org/resources/john-macarthur/criticism-pastors-common-companion/.

satisfaction and influence that drove him, but the spiritual good of the flock of Christ. At the time when he would have been most justified to turn inward, to fall prey to self-pity, to respond to the Corinthians in angry and hurtful words, he rather reasserts his whole-souled commitment to sacrificially serve them in spite of their response.

Facing a similar situation in the Galatian churches, Paul asked, "Am I therefore become your enemy, because I tell you the truth?" (Gal. 4:16). He had lovingly proclaimed the truth to them at great personal cost, but now, through the influence of false teachers, the Galatians had turned in opposition to the apostle and his message. Paul's response is again striking. As a tender father, he continued seeking their welfare. He wrote, "My little children, of whom I travail in birth again until Christ be formed in you" (Gal. 4:19). He was spending himself in agonizing prayer and proclamation. Why? That their hearts might be molded after the image of Christ. Unjust criticism did not deter the apostle from pouring himself out for the church because his vision was consumed with their spiritual vitality, not his own name.

Cornelius Van Til, twentieth-century Reformed Christian, theologian, and apologist, experienced scathing criticism throughout his career. For a number of years the *Calvin Forum*, under the editorship of Cecil De Boer, became the scholarly platform of verbal opposition to Van Til. Unfortunately, much of the critique was anything but scholarly and presented significant misunderstandings of Van Til's thought, even falsely accusing him of teaching a form of philosophical idealism in Christian garb. Van Til's friend and fellow biblical scholar, Philip Edgcumbe Hughes, wrote Van Til in the midst of this controversy:

> What I want you to know is that your labours are, I believe, by
> God's grace, bearing fruit in my life and thinking. I am con-

vinced that your thesis is fundamentally *right,* that is, *scriptural.* The task is to convince others of this, and the main difficulty of this task is the *unwillingness* of other Christians to think so deeply and radically. But we must strive in faith for a new reformation of thinking amongst Christians. Do not doubt that God will prosper us in this purpose. As for the criticisms and misconceptions of those who oppose you, they are for the most part superficial and at times despicable.[8]

What was Hughes doing here? He was seeking to lift the gaze of Van Til above the false accusations and to encourage him that his labors were indeed bearing fruit. He was encouraging him to press on in the midst of great opposition to bring about reformation for the building up of the church. If your faithfulness is bearing fruit in the lives of God's people, who cares if you are opposed? Continue to press on. Lift your vision above yourself and your circumstances and remember the reason why Christ has commissioned you to the ministry in the first place—to serve and build up His people.

Such a church-building vision will pursue not only the spiritual well-being of the church, but the expansion of the church through evangelistic endeavor. Paul, while unjustly suffering in prison, wrote, "Therefore I endure all things for the elect's sakes, that they may also obtain the salvation which is in Christ Jesus with eternal glory" (2 Tim. 2:10). A love for the lost and a zeal to see the kingdom of Christ advanced will enable us to endure the greatest of opposition.

How often we fail to speak to others about Christ because we fear the discomfort of potential verbal opposition. We love our own lives more than the perishing multitudes around us. We

8. Quoted in John R. Muether, *Cornelius Van Til: Reformed Apologist and Churchman* (Phillipsburg, NJ: P&R, 2008), 164.

are content with them heading to eternal destruction so long as we may remain comfortable. But Paul possessed a vision that reached beyond himself—a vision of the elect from every nation, tribe, and tongue. It was a vision that moved him to view every unbeliever as a mission field and emboldened him to endure the greatest opposition both verbally and physically if only those men and women might lay hold of Christ and become the recipients of eternal life in Him.

Pastor, do you possess this church-building vision? Are you laboring in spite of opposition to see your people grow in spiritual maturity and to see the lost brought to a saving knowledge of the truth?

A JUDGMENT-DAY VISION

With the death of Cecil De Boer, the *Calvin Forum* ceased publication. This meant the great platform of verbal opposition to Van Til had collapsed. How did Van Til react? No doubt, there was a sense of relief that this constant barrage of unjust critique would be no more. The mouth of his primary public foe had been silenced. But this was not the grounds of his great consolation. In his private journal, Van Til expressed an entirely different reason for his relief. Commenting on these events, he wrote, "How thankful I now am that I was moderate in expression in reply to his violence. We must always speak as those who may be called to give an account any day."[9] Van Til had shown a persistent humility and submission to the Lord throughout the years of the *Calvin Forum*'s campaign against him. This fostered his relief— not that his enemy was finally silenced, but that he had been kept by the grace of God from responding to De Boer with similar enmity. Why? Because he knew that one day he would stand

9. Quoted in Muether, 173.

before the judgment seat of Christ. He possessed a sober sense of the last day.

Such a judgment-day vision encourages us to maintain a clear conscience before God as we deal with our critics. It enables us, like Van Til, not to respond blow for blow and hate for hate, but rather to love and serve our critics. Brother, we will one day stand before Christ to be judged for every word and every deed we have carried out in the ministry. As pastors we will be judged more strictly. Are we being exemplary in our love toward our critics? Let us take heed lest we speak or act toward them in a way that would mar our conscience and bring shame on judgment day.

A vision of the last day will not only produce a holy watchfulness over our conduct, but it will also bring criticism into its proper perspective. Responding to the opposition of the Corinthians, Paul writes, "But with me it is a very small thing that I should be judged by you or by any human court" (1 Cor. 4:3 ESV). How many of us could say that? To be judged, misunderstood, slandered, or condemned by others is anything but "a very small thing." We are easily consumed by the verdict of a human court. But Paul is not. He is almost entirely indifferent to the matter. He continues, "In fact, I do not even judge myself. For I am not aware of anything against myself, but I am not thereby acquitted" (vv. 3, 4). For Paul even his own clear conscience was not the fundamental ground of his confidence. Who gave the ultimate verdict that mattered? It was God. Paul's consuming concern was not the courtroom of men but the courtroom of God: "It is the Lord who judges me" (v. 4).

Does this nullify the importance of conscience? Absolutely not.[10] Paul drew great confidence from this inner courtroom. He

10. Paul's teaching is pervaded with the importance of conscience. See Acts 23:1; 24:16; Romans 2:15; 9:1; 13:5; 1 Corinthians 8:7–12; 10:25–29; 2 Corinthians 1:12; 4:2; 5:11; 1 Timothy 1:5; 19; 3:9; 4:2; 2 Timothy 1:3; 2:15. For more on conscience in its relation to criticism, see chapter 6.

was unaware of anything against him, and this was a great comfort. But he recognized that his judgment could be skewed and his conscience faulty.

Does this nullify the importance of listening to the criticism of fellow human beings? No. He didn't say that he completely ignored critique and judgment, but rather that the accusations of a human court were "a very small thing" to him. He did not obsess over what others thought of him. Criticism didn't keep him awake at night for weeks on end.

Claim the promise recorded in Isaiah 54:17: "No weapon that is formed against thee shall prosper; and every tongue that shall rise against thee in judgment thou shalt condemn. This is the heritage of the servants of the LORD, and their righteousness is of me, saith the LORD." What a precious text this is. It is Christ's righteousness—not our own—that justifies us as beleaguered servants of Christ.

When I was going through the roughest season of criticism in ministry of my life, this truth was deeply pressed on my conscience. I memorized Isaiah 54:17 and repeated it several times to myself every day for several months. Sometimes I pleaded on it at God's throne with tears; at other times, I spoke it aloud with a sense of joyous ecstasy and victory. Then, when matters became worse instead of better and I was rejected in my denomination, God did something special for me: He had four elders and friends write or call me within a two-week period in my heart-wrenching time of grief to tell me that this very text had been on their mind and heart as they thought of me and prayed for me. The comfort this repeated affirmation gave my soul was beyond human words. It lifted me up above the excruciating pain of rejection and helped me to trust that God had greater things in store for me in terms of usefulness and fruitfulness.

Ultimately, it is God's judgment alone that matters. When our vision is governed by the monumental significance of the final judgment and the divine verdict, we will be enabled to rightly perceive the judgment of conscience and our human critics. Such an eschatological perspective will free us from being consumed with the human courtroom we often find ourselves in. What is the judgment of man in light of the judgment of God?

AN OTHERWORLDLY VISION

A well-written novel will produce a thousand emotions and questions in its readers as they turn its pages. Will the antagonist win the day? How will the problematic plot be resolved? The conflict and tension woven through the story are intended to cause great suspense and consternation. But if you pick up that novel and read it a second time, you will find yourself not nearly as affected. Why? Because you know the end of the story. As you read its many distressing scenes, you recognize that the protagonist will stand victorious in the end. Knowing the final outcome changes the way you engage the story.

God has told us the end of our story. He has gone out of His way to explain the glory that awaits Christians after their momentary suffering here. And this should change the way we view criticism. We know the end. We have hope in the gospel. This future-oriented expectation of blessing in Christ loosens our grip on our reputation, our comfort, and our very life, by reminding us of our heavenly inheritance. It tells us we are pilgrims and ought to expect hardship and opposition here, but great glory to come. It enables us to say with Christ, "Blessed are ye, when men shall revile you, and persecute you, and shall say all manner of evil against you falsely, for my sake. Rejoice, and be exceeding glad: [why?] for great is your reward in heaven" (Matt. 5:11–12). One reason why the scowls of our fellow man have such a crippling affect on us is because we are far too fixated on this present life.

Read of the crushing opposition and tribulation Paul endured (see 2 Cor. 6:4–10; 11:23–29). But for the grace of God, no man could continue in the ministry under such intense tribulations. Yet Paul could describe his backbreaking, soul-agonizing, perpetual afflictions as "light" and "momentary" (2 Cor. 4:17). How? Because he recognized that his suffering for the sake of the gospel was fitting him for "a far more exceeding and eternal weight of glory" (v. 17). He was looking not to the world of sense and time, but to the unseen and eternal world (see v. 18). This brought his present ministerial afflictions into proper perspective.

How much present comfort and strength we forfeit by failing to have this otherworldly perspective. "If in this life only we have hope in Christ, we are of all men most miserable" (1 Cor. 15:19). But this is not the case! In Christ we possess a hope that reaches into the endless ages of eternity. Our hope is in a world of perfect love, a world without criticism! Jonathan Edwards, having exalted in the Triune God of heaven, worshipfully proclaims, "There in heaven this fountain of love, this eternal three in one, is set open without any obstacle to hinder access to it. There this glorious God is manifested and shines forth in full glory, in beams of love; there the fountain overflows in streams and rivers of love and delight, enough for all to drink at, and to swim in, yea, so as to overflow the world as it were with a deluge of love."[11] The world that God is fitting us for is one permeated with and submerged under the measureless love of God.

On the other side of Jordan, our faithful Savior will be waiting for us. Because of Jesus Christ, we will enjoy perfect friendship with the triune God, forever knowing, loving, and communing with the Father, the Son, and the Spirit. As a woman embracing

11. Jonathan Edwards, *The Sermons of Jonathan Edwards: A Reader,* eds. Wilson H. Kimnach, Kenneth P. Minkema, and Douglas A. Sweeney (Yale University Press, 1999), 245. Pastor, you would do well when in the trenches of ministerial hostility to read this famous sermon of Edwards, which is titled "Heaven, A World of Love."

her newborn forgets the pain of delivery, your trials in the ministry will immediately be forgotten in the embrace of Immanuel. He will wipe away every tear from your eyes and will prove to be the Friend who sticks closer than a brother.

Not only will we have perfect communion with God, but also perfect communion with one another. We will commune with the holy angels and the "spirits of just men made perfect" (Heb. 12:23). There will be no denominations, no divisions, no disagreements, no misunderstandings, no theological arguments, and no ignorance. There will not be a hair's breadth of difference among the saints. Even Luther and Calvin, and John Wesley and George Whitefield will agree fully on every point. We shall all be one even as Christ is in the Father and the Father in Him. There will be a complete, perfect, visible, intimate oneness. Our believing critics in this life will embrace us then, and we them. There will be nothing in us worthy of criticism, and no one who possesses the ability to criticize unjustly. All criticism will be silenced forever.

Oh, happy day when this mortality shall put on immortality, and we shall ever be with the Lord! Let all the criticism that our Sovereign God in His infinite wisdom calls us to endure in this life make us more homesick for the criticism-free land of glory. Let our vision be consumed with this world of love, sweetening the often loveless adversity we face here below.

EXEMPLIFY THIS VISION TO YOUR PEOPLE

We conclude with a quote from John Newton, writing to a ministerial friend, John Ryland, as his young wife was on the verge of dying. Listen to his counsel:

How often have we told our hearers, that our all-sufficient and faithful Lord can and will make good every want and loss!

How often have we spoken of the light of his countenance as a full compensation for every suffering, and of the trials of the present life as not worthy to be compared with the exceeding abundant and eternal weight of glory to which they are leading! We must not therefore wonder, if we are sometimes called to exemplify the power of what we have said, and to shew our people that we have not set before them unfelt truths, which we have learnt from books and men only. You are now in a post of honour, and many eyes are upon you. May the Lord enable you to glorify *him*, and to encourage *them*, by your exemplary submission to his will![12]

Brother, in the midst of verbal opposition, let us show our people that we really believe the realities that we proclaim: the God-glorifying, church-building, judgment-day, otherworldly vision of the Scriptures is indeed our vision. That these are not "unfelt truths" that have never moved from our heads to our hearts. That we have owned these biblical bifocals as our own. In the ministerial hostility we face, God is calling us to "exemplify the power" of these stunning doctrines.

So, don't resign from ministry, but *re-sign*, looking unto Jesus, the author and finisher of our faith. Keep your hand on the plow, not looking back, for he that looks back is not fit for the kingdom of God. Fight God's battles, and He will fight yours. And always remember to cling to His promises, especially Isaiah 54:17: "No weapon that is formed against thee shall prosper; and every tongue that shall rise against thee in judgment thou shalt condemn. This is the heritage of the servants of the LORD, and their righteousness is of me, saith the LORD."

12. "A Letter from the Rev. Mr. Newton to a Baptist Minister, Whose Wife Was at the Point of Death" (Jan. 23, 1787), in *The Baptist Magazine for 1821* (London, 1821), 152.

APPENDIX

PREPARING FOR THE FIRES OF CRITICISM WHILE IN SEMINARY

Nick Thompson

As I write this, I am approaching my final semester of seminary, knee-deep in ordination exams, and eagerly anticipating stepping into gospel ministry. To say I am excited to become an under-shepherd of Christ's sheep would be an understatement. My desire for the pastorate, however, is mixed with a significant trepidation of soul. To be honest, sometimes the fear is crippling. What if I don't make it in the ministry? What if the opposition and verbal flak is too much to bear? Stories of pastoral resignation and even suicide abound. I sometimes wonder if my story will be another tragic account added to the list of ministerial failure.

The reality is that academic lectures and research papers offer little help in preparing prospective pastors for the fires of crit-icism. Yet the seminary environment is, by God's good design, an ideal training ground for cultivating the inner strength of soul needed to survive and thrive in the furnace of pastoral opposi-tion. But it will take great intentionality.

It is toward this end that I offer the Seminarian's Deca-logue—ten things to avoid in seminary in order to prepare for long-term endurance in gospel ministry. Why focus on don'ts instead of dos? For the same reason that God gave the original Decalogue in an almost entirely prohibitory form. Sinclair Ferguson explains that through the stone tablets given at Sinai "God was republishing his original blueprint for life. But now it was 'contextualised' or applied to the *sitz im leben,* the life-setting of sinners. Its negative cast had the goal of preventing them from further self-destruction."[1] The hearts of twenty-first-century seminarians are no less idolatrous than the hearts of ancient Israelites. Given the *sitz im leben* of sinful seminarians, I offer ten prohibitions for seminary life that if heeded will go a long way toward preparing us for ministerial criticism.

1. DON'T NEGLECT YOUR SOUL

This may seem like an obvious point to begin with, but it cannot be stressed too strongly.[2] The sarcastic equating of sem-inaries with cemeteries is unfortunately not far from the truth in too many cases. The academic study of the Bible and theology can have a deadening effect on our souls if we are not diligent in our pursuit of Christ and Christlikeness. If you allow your soul to shrivel up through the seminary years, you will not be fit for the crosses of pastoral ministry. A soul steeled with strength is a soul that is experientially acquainted with God and His Word.

Set aside time each day to commune with God in the Scrip-tures and prayer, and guard it jealously. Don't allow the pressures of seminary life to swallow up your pursuit of the Lord. If you

---

1. Sinclair B. Ferguson, *Devoted to God: Blueprints for Sanctification* (Edin-burgh: Banner of Truth Trust, 2016), 167.
2. See David Mathis and Jonathan Parnell, *How to Stay Christian in Semi-nary* (Wheaton, IL: Crossway, 2014).

think the weights you are carrying now are heavy, just wait until you get in the ministry! Learn to place the highest of premiums on the secret place. And plead with God that He might daily open your eyes to behold more of His glory in His Word.

The great temptation for me as a student has not been to completely disregard the meditative study of the Word and prayer, but for seminary to creep into these holy exercises. I am assigned an exegesis paper on Malachi 1, and suddenly for the next two weeks my daily devotions are spent studying the Hebrew minutiae of this minor prophet. Don't fall prey to this. You need to feast on God's Word for no other purpose than to feed your soul. Don't make your devotions a means to the end of completing a paper, project, or sermon. The end of the secret place is intimate communion with God. Seek it as if your soul depends on it—because it does! Failure here will surely lead to a deficiency in the God-fearing humility necessary to bear up under verbal flak in the ministry.

2. DON'T NEGLECT YOUR BODY

God has not crafted us to be disembodied spirits. Each us of, writes John Murray, is a "psychosomatic being."[3] We are the result of a divinely constructed, mysterious interconnection of body and soul. This wedding together of the physical and spiritual means that "the health of the body affects the health of the soul and vice versa."[4] In other words, given our body-soul makeup as image-bearing creatures, we cannot neglect our physical health without it having significant negative psychological and spiritual effects.

There are three primary ingredients to pursuing and maintaining physical health. First, your body needs consistent,

3. John Murray, "Trichotomy," in *Collected Writings of John Murray* (Edinburgh: Banner of Truth Trust, 1977), 2:33.
4. David Murray, *Reset: Living a Grace-Paced Life in a Burnout Culture* (Wheaton, IL: Crossway, 2017), 41.

uninterrupted sleep, preferably seven to eight hours a night. Train your body by keeping a regular bedtime and wake-up time. Do not give in to the temptation to pull an all-nighter to study for that exam. It is not worth it. If you are dependent on coffee to keep you awake in class, you are not getting enough sleep. Second, your body needs a nutritious diet. Seminary students, typically living on a small budget, tend to eat very poorly. It is probably not realistic to begin eating all organic and unprocessed foods, but seek to eat as healthy as possible. No more ramen noodles and high fructose corn syrup. Third, your body needs exercise. Build a stand-up desk to prevent yourself from sitting for ten hours a day while studying. If it is possible to ride a bike to class, do so rather than driving a car. Along with this, find some way to really sweat three or even four days a week. I use a rigorous body-weight exercise program that requires no equipment or gym membership.

Temptations abound to compromise our physical health in seminary, but we must not give in to them. While it might sound strange, you will lack the strength of soul needed to endure ministerial criticism if you are failing to care for your body. If you don't believe me, spend a week sleeping no more than four or five hours a night and eating nothing but junk food and see how it affects your walk with the Lord, your emotions, and your ability to handle life's problems.[5]

3. DON'T DISCOUNT THE LOCAL CHURCH

It is ironic that men training to serve the church often spend their seminary years neglecting the church. A churchless

---

5. For a helpful overall treatment of this subject, see Albert N. Martin, *Glorifying God in Your Body: Whose is It—Yours or His?* (Montville, NJ: Trinity Pulpit Press, 2015).

seminarian is a contradiction of terms. Without any serious attachment to a local congregation in our years of preparation, we will lack the fitness requisite to survive and thrive in future pastoral ministry. Denny Burk writes, "The [seminarians] that tend to flame out in ministry are the ones whose connection to the local church is very loose."[6]

When we moved to Grand Rapids for seminary, my wife and I recognized that we could easily spend a year visiting all the different churches in the area. But after the first month, we had our sights set on Harvest Orthodox Presbyterian Church. We became members a couple months later, and I am so thankful we did! Spending the seminary years bouncing around from church to church, never getting close to anyone or serving in any consistent way or submitting under God-ordained leadership via church membership, is one of the most serious mistakes a future pastor can make in this season. Excuses are made for lack of involvement in a local church. Perhaps you are a member of a church back home. Or you find it helpful to visit different churches to broaden your ecclesiastical horizons. Or you can't find a church that fits your particular preferences. But I question whether there is ever a legitimate excuse for a seminarian not to commit himself as an active member in a local body of believers.

The local church is one of God's greatest instruments to deflate the puffed-up egos of arrogant seminarians.[7] As you seek to use your gifts to serve God's people, many will appreciate you. But there will most likely be some who won't. There will also be those who love you enough to help you see the areas where you need to grow. Some will do this gently, others gruffly, but all of it

6. Denny Burk, "Don't Do Seminary Without the Church," April 1, 2012, https://www.dennyburk.com/dont-do-seminary-without-the-church/.
7. If you think you are not arrogant, heed the words of C. S. Lewis: "If you think you are not conceited, it means you are very conceited indeed" (*Mere Christianity* [New York: Harper Collins, 2001], 128).

is working toward your growth in humility—a humility you will need if you are to survive ministerial opposition.

4. DON'T LOSE SIGHT OF WHO YOU ARE

Much of my seminary experience has consisted in the painful realization that my self-image is grounded in what I accomplish, rather than in gospel privilege. My heart is quick to derive my self-worth from what I do—the grades I get, the positions I obtain, the books I read, the affirmations I receive. I am quick to compare myself to fellow students and prospective ministers, establishing my value on the vain thought that I am a better preacher or a better thinker or a better whatever. But if my worth is found in earthly successes and the praise of man, what will happen when I fail or when I am opposed? What will happen when a fellow student possesses a stronger intellect or a greater giftedness in preaching?

Such a pride-induced, man-inflated identity is sure to self-destruct. And praise God for that! For after our self-constructed image is irreparably shattered, we may be inclined to seek our identity in the gospel. This we must do! As I look back over my past three years in seminary, not a single lesson I learned is more vital than this: to daily find my identity, value, and purpose in Jesus Christ alone. This is a battle, and as such, it requires unremitted preaching of the gospel to oneself.

When we think of our identity in the Son of God, we cannot fail to consider all the salvific blessings that come to us through our union with Christ. But perhaps none so decimates the idolatrous identities we construct as the gift of adoption. J. I. Packer calls adoption "the highest privilege that the gospel offers: higher even than justification."[8] What a statement!

8. J. I. Packer, *Knowing God* (Downers Grove, IL: InterVarsity Press,

And it doesn't take long to realize why Packer would make it. To know God, not merely as a Judge whose righteous demands have been met, but as a warm-hearted Father who lavishes His eternal love on us, is nothing short of astounding. Study the doctrine of adoption. Meditate on your privileges as a son of God. The Westminster Confession of Faith sets forth many of these household blessings. Here they are in personalized form with the original proof texts:

- I have God's name put on me (see Jer. 14:9; 2 Cor. 6:18; Rev. 3:12).
- I receive the Spirit of adoption (see Rom. 8:15).
- I have access to the throne of grace with boldness (see Rom. 5:2; Eph. 3:12).
- I am enabled to cry, "Abba, Father" (see Gal. 4:6).
- I am pitied (see Gal. 4:6), protected (see Prov. 14:26), and provided for (see Matt. 6:30, 32; 1 Peter 5:7) by God my Father.
- I am chastened by God my Father (see Heb. 12:6), yet never cast off (see Lam. 3:31).
- I am sealed to the day of redemption (see Eph. 4:30) and inherit the promises (see Heb. 6:12) as an heir of everlasting salvation (see Heb. 1:14; 1 Peter 1:3, 4).

Such a knowledge of sonship in Christ will deliver you from "the world's anxious quest to 'be somebody.'"[9] You are somebody! If you are in Christ, you are an eternally loved child of God, not because of your gifts or accomplishments, but because of the good pleasure and free grace of God.

1973), 206.

9. Sinclair B. Ferguson, *Children of the Living God: Delighting in the Father's Love* (Edinburgh: Banner of Truth, 1989), 51.

5. DON'T LIVE FOR A 4.0

God often uses our failures to lovingly remind us of our identity in Christ. I had one such moment after writing an essay for Reformation Church History on Calvin's doctrine of the Lord's Supper. I poured myself into this paper, carefully crafting each sentence and packing its footnotes with primary and secondary sources. I was dreaming of publishing it in a theological journal someday. But there was one problem—I had a slight misunderstanding of Calvin's position. And it cost me, dropping my grade for the class to an A–. My perfect 4.0 GPA suddenly became a 3.98! How could I live with myself? Perhaps it would not have been so embarrassing to get an A– in Medieval Church History, but Reformation Church History? That ought to be my bread and butter. Yet here I was with my perfectionistic dream of straight As dashed to the ground.

I came to realize that my blunder was a gracious intervention of God, exposing the hidden layers of pride in my heart. Why was I so devastated by an A-? I wanted the significance of being at the top of my class, the approval of my professors, and the esteem of my fellow students. "We desire perfection," writes Amy Baker, "as a means to be accepted or to control our fear of rejection or failure."[10] My perfect GPA was a means of *controlling* my innate fear of being viewed by others as an unsuccessful blockhead. Left unmortified, such perfectionism and fear of failure would have proven to be lethal in future gospel ministry.

You and I will fail as pastors. We will preach bad sermons. We will attempt new things that will flop. We will give unwise counsel. These things are inevitable. The only impeccable shepherd is Jesus Christ! Don't wait to learn this lesson until you get into

10. Amy Baker, *Picture Perfect: When Life Doesn't Line Up* (Greensboro, NC: New Growth Press, 2014), 38.

gospel ministry. Embrace your failures now. Allow them to humble you and drive you to the perfect Savior of imperfect sinners. If we center our lives on the pursuit of perfection in seminary, we will be devastated when our future congregation quickly realizes that we are less than perfect and tells us so.

6. DON'T PRETEND YOU ARE OMNISCIENT

This point is intimately related to the last, but it warrants a separate prohibition. The reason you are in seminary is because you don't know everything. Don't pretend like you do. Too often I have sought to appear as the expert on Owen's pneumatology, Van Til's apologetic methodology, Newton's pastoral counsel, and Vos's eschatology all in the same breath! Too often I have fled discussions that focused on topics I was not knowledgeable of because I didn't want to appear intellectually inferior. Too often I have failed to ask questions in the classroom out of a fear of looking dumb. At all costs, I have avoided the dreaded words, "I don't know."

Can I encourage you to embrace those words? Seminary is a safe place to have them regularly on your tongue. No one expects you to know everything as a student, but some will expect a knowledge just short of omniscience when you are a pastor. If you don't learn how to admit your ignorance now, you will be in big trouble in future ministry. Sooner or later, your ignorance will be exposed.

7. DON'T RUN FROM CONSTRUCTIVE CRITIQUE

Seminary is the prime time to run *toward* constructive criticism. Don't avoid it; seek after it. Out of all of my seminary courses, I learned the most from practice preaching. During each class a different student preaches a sermon, followed by a critique from professors and fellow students. I grew in leaps and bounds from this class, not because of the sermons preached, but because of the criticism given. Books on preaching and general homiletic courses are helpful, but there is nothing quite like having a seasoned preacher tear apart your sermon. As painful as criticism is, there is no way around the fact that it is one of the primary methods the Lord uses to grow and teach us. So learn to embrace it during the seminary years.

Find a godly older man in your church who is willing to mentor you. Don't ask someone who will tell you what you want to hear, but someone who will tell you what you need to hear. Find a man who will lovingly challenge you to grow. Open your heart to him, warts and all. Seek out his counsel and prayers.

8. DON'T COMPROMISE IN SMALL THINGS

More than an intellectual training ground, seminary is a moral proving ground. The all-encompassing ethical characteristic you must possess to be qualified for eldership is to be "blameless" (1 Tim. 3:2; Titus 1:7). Emblazon that on your mind! Seek to be above reproach in every regard by God's grace. If we would have strength to endure verbal opposition later, we must maintain a clear conscience before God now.[11]

Charles Hodge warned his seminary students, "When a present gratification can be attained by a violation of strict integrity not sufficiently serious to shock the conscience, or endanger the reputation, the temptation is yielded to without hesitation."[12] Hodge's words are convicting and true! We are most prone to

---

11. I encourage you to go back and read the more extensive treatment of conscience as it relates to criticism in chapter 6.

12. Charles Hodge, "The Character Traits of the Gospel Minister," in *Princeton and the Work of the Christian Ministry,* ed. James M. Garretson, vol. 2 (Edinburgh: Banner of Truth Trust, 2012), 134.

moral compromise when we can get away with it without our internal alarm (conscience) or external alarms (other people) sounding. Such sinful gratification can take any number of forms: A slight exaggeration to make a point. A half-hearted laziness while writing a paper. A mild form of plagiarism. A second glance at an inappropriate ad. Two-too-many pieces of pizza. We must strive in dependence on the Spirit of Christ to keep these things from having a place in our lives.

Examine yourself before the mirror of God's law. Are their areas of compromise in your life, even if they be small? Resolve to put these things to death and to cultivate the Spirit-wrought boldness that comes from living under the smile of God with a conscience washed in the blood of Christ. The things you click on in your internet browser, the way you spend your time and money, and the integrity of your speech are all intimately related to how you will handle future opposition in the ministry.

9. DON'T BE ASHAMED OF THE GOSPEL

The gospel of Jesus Christ is politically incorrect, and North American culture is growing increasingly antipathetic to it. Rico Tice describes the Christian message as "incendiary."[13] If you don't know what that means, neither did I. The dictionary defines it as "designed to cause fires." The gospel, by the all-wise design of God, is fire-producing. It will cause uproar and offense. It will divide families. It will spark violent hatred. It will turn friends into enemies. Therefore, preaching the gospel provides us with a wonderful opportunity to suffer verbal hostility for righteousness sake.

I have found it incredibly easy to make excuses not to engage my neighbors with gospel-saturated hospitality or not to go out

---

13. Rico Tice with Carl Laferton, *Honest Evangelism: How to Talk about Jesus Even When It's Tough* (Epsom, UK: The Good Book Company, 2015), 17.

on the streets with fellow brothers to engage people with the truth. *I am far too busy*, I tell myself. And seminary *is* a demanding season of life, especially if you are married and working a job on the side. But if I am too busy to evangelize, it is not evangelism that needs to go, but something else. I am training to be a minister of the gospel. How can a man preparing for gospel ministry be too busy to share the gospel? The fact is that most of the time my busyness excuse is actually a cover-up for a deep-seated fear. My neighbors might think I'm weird. People on the street might call me names. I might not know the answer to an objection, and I would look like a fool. These fears reveal an obsession with myself and what others think of me.

Learn to count it all joy "when others revile you and persecute you and utter all kids of evil against you falsely on [Christ's] account" (Matt. 5:11 ESV). Learn to "share in suffering for the gospel by the power of God" (2 Tim. 1:8 ESV). Through the opposition we face in evangelism, God is thickening our skin for what we will face after ordination.

10. DON'T FORGET WHY YOU ARE HERE

We must have it clear in our minds why we have come to seminary in the first place. To what end has God called us to devote these years to study? The obvious answer is to build up His church. The reason you are training to be an under-shepherd is "to equip the saints for the work of ministry, for building up the body of Christ, until we all attain to the unity of the faith and of the knowledge of the Son of God, to mature manhood, to the measure of the stature of the fullness of Christ" (Eph. 4:12–13 ESV).

It is easy to lose sight of this. How many, including myself, have come to seminary ready to spend themselves in gospel ministry for the sake of the church, only to find themselves quickly starry-eyed with the thought of PhDs and professorships. Let me be clear: there is a place for advanced degrees and professors, but the primary purpose of the seminary is to train pastors. Don't be easily diverted from this path. Don't forget that the purpose of the pastorate is to build and perfect the body of Christ. You are giving yourself to rigorous study in seminary, not to make a name for yourself, not to become a best-selling author or celebrity conference speaker, but to serve the church.

This truth is liberating. It frees us from our native desire to be approved, applauded, esteemed, and honored. This is not about us. It has never been about us. We exist, are in seminary, and will, if it pleases the Lord, enter into the ministry for no other purpose than to pour ourselves out for Christ's bride.

CONCLUSION

In 1651, the Church of Scotland published a document titled *A Humble Acknowledgement of the Sins of the Ministry of Scotland.* It is a heart-searching, humbling confession of the sin and compromise present among these seventeenth-century Scottish Presbyterian pastors. It includes, however, not only a confession of sins concerning those in the ministry, but also those preparing for the ministry. One such confession is this: "Not studying self-denial, nor resolving to take up the Cross of CHRIST."[14] These men grieved the fact that those training for the pastorate were not learning to identify with Christ in His humiliation. They weren't learning the cross.

In one way or another, the ten prohibitions given above could be summarized in a singular positive precept: "Deny yourself, take up your cross, and follow Christ." There is no other God-honoring way to endure the fires of future ministerial critique.

14. Quoted in Horatius Bonar, *Words to Winners of Souls* (Pensacola, FL: Chapel Library, 2000), 16.

Realistic preparation for ministry can go a long way toward easing a new pastor's make-or-break first year. Drawing on decades of pastoral experience, Charles Wingard gives you the essentials and provides the real-world help needed for navigating the primary duties of the minister: from sermon preparation and sacraments to visitation, counseling, and hospitality. Get the tools you need to establish you in your ministry and lead with confidence.

"This book is simply excellent—extremely practical and exceedingly wise. The writing is clear, direct, and full of good sense, just as I would expect from Pastor Wingard."
    —**Kevin DeYoung**

"I cannot conceive of anyone from whom I would rather receive counsel on the practice of the Christian ministry. Needless to say then, I am thrilled that he has written *Help for the New Pastor*. Even if you have been in the ministry for a long time, there are things to be learned and relearned here. I have. You will too."
    —**Ligon Duncan**

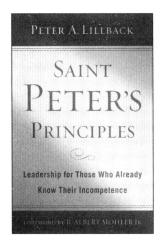

In this comprehensive handbook, Peter Lillback, president of Westminster Theological Seminary, uses the apostle Peter's life and writings to guide men and women through the details and daily challenges of leadership in any arena. Readers will think through their relationships, productivity, management style, communication, decision-making, conflict resolution, integrity, and more. Practical spiritual exercises help to put the lessons of each short section into action.

"This is a rich, wonderfully instructive and helpful compendium of wisdom on all aspects of leadership. There is nothing merely theoretical."
    —**Alistair Begg**

"I have never read a book on leadership quite like this one. . . . Peter Lillback's book is a treasure-house of wisdom to be digested slowly."
    —**D. A. Carson**

MORE PASTORAL RESOURCES FROM P&R PUBLISHING

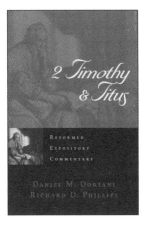

"Godly living and faithful leadership require tremendous grace in this corrupt world. How is it possible? Doriani and Phillips give us solid expositions of the divinely inspired directions in Paul's second epistle to Timothy and his epistle to Titus. Read and grow, and use your gifts and prayers to promote godly leadership."
—**Joel R. Beeke**

The Reformed Expository Commentary (REC) series is accessible to both pastors and lay readers. Each volume in the series provides exposition that gives careful attention to the biblical text, is doctrinally Reformed, focuses on Christ through the lens of redemptive history, and applies the Bible to our contemporary setting.

Praise for the Reformed Expository Commentary Series

"Well-researched and well-reasoned, practical and pastoral, shrewd, solid, and searching."
—**J. I. Packer**

"A rare combination of biblical insight, theological substance, and pastoral application."
—**Al Mohler**

ALSO BY JOEL R. BEEKE

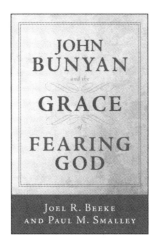

He was the author of the best-selling Christian book of all time. His Bible-saturated works have inspired generations of believers all over the world. And yet, as influential as it is, John Bunyan's theology contains a unifying thread that is sorely neglected in the modern church: the vital importance of the fear of God.

Fearing God is seen by many as psychologically harmful—at odds with belief in a God of love. But Bunyan knew personally that the only freedom from a guilty fear of God's wrath is a joyful, childlike fear of his holiness. Joel Beeke and Paul Smalley guide us through Bunyan's life before exploring his writings to illuminate the true grace of fearing God.

"Wisdom requires it, Jesus emphasized it, the apostles encouraged it— and yet few things are more feared in contemporary Christianity than . . . the fear of God. This timely book . . . shows how the fear of God was, in contrast, the heartbeat of one of the most loved and admired of all Christians."
    —Sinclair B. Ferguson

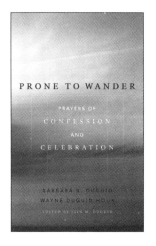 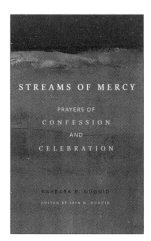

Confessing our sins might seem like a gloomy business . . . but exposing the specifics of our struggles with sin leads to celebration! It points us back to the good news of the gospel, our great Savior, and our forgiveness through God's grace.

Inspired by the Puritan classic *The Valley of Vision*, the prayers in these two volumes are ideal for use in church services or personal devotions. They open with a scriptural call of confession, confess specific sins, thank the Father for Jesus's perfect life and death in our place, ask for the help of the Spirit in pursuing holiness, and close with an assurance of pardon.

"[*Prone to Wander*] has many virtues. . . . The book covers the whole of the Christian life. I love its overall aims and method."
   —Leland Ryken

"Here we learn how to pray God's Word back to him . . . and celebrate his grace in so many areas of our lives. I recommend [*Streams of Mercy*] strongly."
   —John Frame

Did you find this book helpful?
Consider writing a review online.
The authors appreciate your feedback!

Or write to P&R at editorial@prpbooks.com
with your comments. We'd love to hear from you.